PALLADIO AND AMERICA

SELECTED PAPERS PRESENTED TO THE CENTRO INTERNAZIONALE DI STUDI DI ARCHITETTURA

ANDREA PALLADIO

TRANSLATED INTO ENGLISH FOR THE CENTER FOR PALLADIAN STUDIES IN AMERICA

1997

MARTIN~ST. MARTIN PUBLISHING COMPANY
NEW ORLEANS

PALLADIO AND AMERICA

SELECTED PAPERS PRESENTED TO
THE CENTRO INTERNAZIONALE
DI STUDI DI ARCHITETTURA

ANDREA PALLADIO

TRANSLATED INTO ENGLISH FOR
THE CENTER FOR PALLADIAN STUDIES
IN AMERICA

Translator: Robert de Lucca
Editor: Christopher Weeks
Copy edited by Jane Powers Weldon.
Designed and produced for
Martin~St. Martin Publishing Company
by Van Jones Martin.

Library of Congress Catalog Card Number: 97–72904

ISBN 0-932958-18-4

Printed in the United States of America

Cover: Mount Airy, Richmond County, Virginia; drawn for the Historic American Buildings Survey.

THE CENTER FOR PALLADIAN STUDIES IN AMERICA, a nonprofit organization, incorporated under the laws of the Commonwealth of Virginia, has been established for the purpose of studying Andrea Palladio and "Palladianism" in the United States.

Andrea Palladio, one of the greatest masters of Renaissance culture, has had an enduring influence on American architecture; his theories were introduced to this country in the mid eighteenth century at such pioneering monuments as Drayton Hall in South Carolina and Mount Airy in Virginia. Later, architects including Peter Harrison, William Buckland, John Trumbull, and Thomas Jefferson began to incorporate forms and motifs from Palladio's great opus, *The Four Books of Architecture*

The Center for Palladian Studies in America will seek to define what "Palladianism" means in an American context and how American buildings are "Palladian," and to present these findings to the public through seminars, lectures, and publications.

Membership to the Center is open to all; dues are $30 for a single membership, $15 for students, and $50 for families. Additional contributions are very acceptable. All dues and contributions are fully tax deductible.

The Center for Palladian Studies in America
13813 Village Mill Drive
Midlothian, VA 23113
804/794-6225; FAX 804/379-5262

CONTENTS

PREFACE AND ACKNOWLEDGMENTS

Since 1959 our sister organization, the Centro Inernazionale di Studi di Architettura Andrea Palladio in Vicenza, has been sponsoring annual conferences of distinguished scholars and has published the papers presented in its yearly *Bollettino*.

Over the years these essays have covered every topic from architecture pre Palladio to his continuing influence up to the present time in places as diverse as Poland, Ireland, and Virginia. Included are articles on the esthetics of Palladio and an analysis of the typographic layout of the *Quattro Libri*.

As orchestrated by Mario di Valmarana, our vice president, The Centro has graciously given permission for us to translate, publish, and make available to the American architectural and scholarly communities some of these papers. We thank Prof. Renato Cevese, Prof. Guido Beltramini, Prof. Giuseppina Dal Santo, and Sig.ra Maria Vittoria Pellizzari, all associated with the Centro, for their assistance in this project.

Our associate, Christopher Weeks, has chosen the following eight articles for their relevance to American Palladianism and has arranged for their translation into English by Robert de Lucca of the Johns Hopkins University Center for Hispanic and Italian Studies. All photographs and other illustrations are copyright by the Centro; we thank various sources for them, including CISA in Vicenza, the Correr Museum in Venice, Yale University's Paul Mellon Center for British Art, Diego Birelli, Foto Boruli in Venice, Foto Tapparo-Trentin in Vicenza, Foto Rossi in Venice, and the Massachusetts Historical Society.

Edmund A. Rennolds, Jr.
President,
Center for Palladian Studies in America

PALLADIO AND AMERICA

THE FOUR BOOKS

The task of highlighting the exceptional originality and expressive quality of the typographic layout of Palladio's *Quattro Libri* falls to me instead of to others merely because, during the last fifty years, scholars have conducted intense and erudite philological discussions about the text and neglected the book as a work of art. In my first study,[1] I indeed limited myself to the graphical aspects of the treatise, although I discussed them from the same point of view as others, that is, looking at Palladian images as a collection of architectural testimonies that might be more or less faithful reports of the buildings reported therein. Unfortunately, the frustration of not being able to distinguish real architectural history from summary declarations or variants, of which Bertotti-Scamozzi also complains, kept me from treating the book as a pure work of art in itself, instead of only as commentary and illustration of precious material.

It is also true that a rigorous analysis of a series of engravings can be carried out only with some knowledge of the technology employed, especially when—as in the present case—one wishes to attribute a different meaning than that suggested by immediate visual evidence. If one lacks that knowledge, it may happen, as we have pointed out elsewhere,[2] that the document is misinterpreted or a compositional variant is even taken for positive representation.

All scholars have bemoaned the insufficiency of detail in the *Quattro Libri*, due to the small scale of the images. This concerns especially the houses, which are not accompanied, as are the larger buildings, by enlarged details. The publication of what nevertheless turned out to be a masterpiece of typography was not funded as liberally as was the edition of the treatise of Cesariano, in 1521, or the later ones of Serlio. But it was these very limits imposed on dimension and quality that stimulated the author to adopt a form of composition in which economy of means translates into artistic wealth, even though the small size means that sufficient detail is lacking in the drawings.

In addition, the marks traced on wood by the graver are inevitably thicker than those engraved on copper plate. Etching also would have

allowed a variation in the line thickness and would have permitted finer
shading through crosshatching. The copperplate engravings in Giacomo
Leoni's 1715 edition of Palladio, printed in London, offer an example of 1.1
this more flexible medium. As has been noted, the interpretation of the
original prints is mediocre in its detail, but the overall effect is finer than 1.2
that of the 1570 edition, with its wood engravings of Palladio's original
drawings. All in all, the greater linear simplicity and sketchiness of the 1.3
xylography in the illustrated books of the Renaissance give them a unique intensity. The chief example of this is the *Hypnerotomachia Poliphili*, the famous masterpiece next to which the *Quattro Libri* may be placed for the layout of its pages, similar in the disposition of black and white areas to the architectural use of space. The woodcut image is continually blended with the text thanks to a common linear effect—in other words, to the constant visibility of the white background within the illustrated page. This is in contrast to copper engraving, which gives an effect of being self-contained because of the higher shading of the chiaroscuro.

To speak of the relationship between black and white on the page, however, comparing it to the architectural use of empty and filled space, is to create something more than a simple creative analogy between typography and architecture. It means that both are defined by their capacity to articulate geometric rhythm, along three dimensions for spatial forms and two for those contained on the level page. All architects believe intuitively that the same faculty that allows for the construction of a building comes into play even during the fashioning of the most simple printed page. I believe, therefore, that architectural schools should assume the task of training pupils in the more difficult and complex applications of typography, which after all is one of the most significant pursuits in modern and industrial design.

In my second essay I should have gone further into the artistic value of the *Quattro Libri*, since the subject, being new, might have covered an entire chapter. A discussion of the novelty of invention and artistic value of certain pages might have ensued, and a comparison with previous treatises, especially those of Serlio (who anticipated Palladio's use of the ratio between text, figure, and title and the blank page), might have been made.

Be that as it may, it seems a good idea to repeat what I said seven years ago:

We must consider the spatial relationship between the letters

> and the prints as something that must have engaged the artist when he laid out the page. In other words, the drawing prepared for printing was assigned to a predetermined surface, filling, for example, the entire facing page with text, or with the text occupying the upper part of the page. Thus the entire plan of a house would sometimes be summarized by a schematic drawing and façade, often with one contained in the other to save space. The prints and the text alternated according to a rhythm that the artist must have established personally. And the same imaginative temperament that disposes the blanks and the images on the page determines the volumes of an actual building.

Perhaps other treatise writers before Palladio acted in the same manner for the definitive version of their work, disposing the text and drawing so that the typographer merely had to translate the ensemble onto the proportions of the page. The manuscript of Serlio's *Sesto Libro* was done in this way, and it is a model of descriptive clarity that seems a finished draft done precisely in view of the final printing.[3] We will speak of this book later on. For now the other books by the Bolognian writer of treatises, known by Palladio, are more important. They also were more widely known than the graphic work of a Fra Giocondo or a Cesariano, probably because of their figurative complexity and clarity of presentation. Serlio's treatise allows us a better comparison with the *Quattro Libri* than does the work of Pietro Cattaneo, closer in time to Palladio, but not composed with the same balance between text and figure that does honor to the tradition furthered by the *Sogno* of Polifilio.

The important elements for Serlio are utility and clarity of representation. I mean that the architecture of the page interests him only in functional terms and not as artistic composition per se. This agrees with his desire to
1.4 furnish the greatest number of architectural details, with equally copious textual comment which, lacking page space, he does not hesitate to slip into the figures themselves. Thus there is sometimes a confused pictorial mass, which, however, is not without its own functional order and suggestiveness. The proximity of text and illustration expresses the enthusiastic fervor with which the author has managed his demonstration, almost as if he were assembling the items in front of the reader's eyes. See, for instance, the plans of the Colosseum in the *Terzo Libro* (*Delle Antichità*, "*Of Antiquities*") with

captions ingeniously placed wherever they will fit, or carved into the drawn blocks of stone that serve as steps, or else arced along the length of the cavea. The four plans, each occupying a quarter of an ellipse, are laid out around dense rectangular captions inserted on the perimeter of the arena. Note also that the large overall plan of the Colosseum (like that of the amphitheater of Verona on page 83) occupies two entire pages, without a break for the binding of the book, so that the design is partially hidden and the whole appears cramped. Palladio, instead, has divided similar images into two distinct engravings, conveniently distanced one from the other (see the Rialto bridge, the temples of Mars the Avenger and of Anthony and Faustina 1.5
in the Pantheon) so that everything is clearer and the page more balanced.

Differences in the use of perspective in the books of Serlio and Palladio are also notable. In his second book, Serlio offers an ample treatise on perspective, and most of the illustrations, from the third to the fifth, are indeed in perspective, so that the cornices are foreshortened, as in many Renaissance drawings, the most famous being those of Palladio and Michelangelo. In these, however, three-dimensional representation serves to point out the measurements for each dimension, while in Serlio perspective is there for pure effect, as with the central perspectives of his buildings, bridges, portals, and chimneys.

For the most part, Palladio does without perspective, except for some very rare occasions when it appears necessary in order to simplify and reduce the number of figures rather than to increase them with an overview. See, for example, the first drawing on page 12 and the three on page 13: in all four, the use of central perspective helps show the internal sections of the wall structure in their link with the face. In this way Palladio avoids having to provide further plan or section illustrations to supplement those present. The fifth and last example is the bridge on the Rhine (III, pages 12–14). The view from above makes it so the wooden structure 1.6
is immediately and intuitively grasped. The author here interprets a text from Cesare, and the perspective helps to reduce the numerous drawings of the layout, section, and prospect that would have been necessary had Palladio not simply supplied some indication regarding the mortises (L, K, I, M, H). The perspective renders the whole structure visible at once.

In terms of typography, a comparison between the two treatises shows that Serlio, though he had a larger page on which to work, does not maintain a constant ratio, as do the *Quattro Libri*, between text and figure. In fact he gives the impression that the space was not large enough for him, renouncing as he does any rhythm whatsoever. Palladio, on the contrary—apart from some differences of a few millimeters, due to the work of the engravers[4]—contains his full-page illustrations within a rectangle of about 270 by 175 millimeters, in such a way that the architectural images are made part of a rhythm that is in itself architectonic and that agrees with his injunction to "get rid of the strange abuses, barbarous inventions and unnecessary expense."

Now, my desire is not to disparage Serlio, whose disinterested and
enthusiastic genius for presentation is very admirable, but it seems to me
that a comparison of his drawing of an Ionic column, compared with that
1.7 of Palladio, proves my point.[5] An example is the drawing of Serlio (IV, page
160) with its three separated elements, unmatched geometrically and
devoid of projection, although the page size would permit a complete
graphical presentation. In addition, the chiaroscuro acts as filler, accentuat-
ing the ornaments at the expense of the main design. Palladio's drawing (I,
1.8 page 34) is wholly linear and perhaps constitutes the best example we have
of economy in architectural representation, since, while it gives a complete
description of detail, it transcends the aim of the illustration itself in an
admirable arabesque that is produced by the juxtaposition and intersection
of the curves and segments, which not only does not detract from the clarity of the figure, but demonstrates the unity of the parts. Even the caption
"the eye of the Volute in large form" finds a place at the upper left; it is the
circle that contains the key for the tracing of the volute and that is repeated,
in smaller form, in the volute itself. On the basis of this, I think it is no
exaggeration to say that the descriptive design not only perfectly accords
with Palladio's genius, but also represents, as a work of art, one of his major
accomplishments insofar as it produces the same joy in contemplation as
does his architecture.

Finally, some peculiarities of the Palladian page are worth considering, in particular those in which the vertical ratio between image and text is established. Serlio also anticipated this type of ratio in his five books, while the sixth, *Delle habitationi di tutti li gradi degli uomini fuori delle città*, in its printed form, did not present a variety of detail, limited as it is (according to the custom of alternating pages of text with pages of illustration) to plans and perspectives, without detail, which had already been set out in the five preceding books, in the form already mentioned.

The typographic composition of the *Quattro Libri* is uniform throughout, except in one place, the frontispiece. This incongruity must not have been desired, but rather tolerated, by Palladio. It can be justified only in terms of advertising, so out of keeping is it with the classic reserve and balance of the rest of the book, including the typographical composition, which recalls the best examples of Aldo in the use of lines of capital letters, although the fonts used are not the same. These capital letters are spaced like inscriptions on stone, used to begin the paragraphs, and varied in line and kerning. The author performs all this while reducing the drawings of his own houses to a minimum size on the page, dedicating much more space to the Vitruvian examples than to his own work.[6]

To comment on another model of impagination, let us look at the vertical compositions I have mentioned. The figures are almost always placed horizontally, one above another, except for some bridges (III, pages 23, 29), and positioned in keeping with the height of the page, clearly in order not to sacrifice detail, something that Palladio has instead not hesitated to do for some of his houses, which even grow into caricatures through extreme graphic reduction, as in the examples of the Maser, the Poiana, and the Thiene at Quinto.

Yet it is in the illustrations of the houses that Palladio achieves utmost
beauty, resorting to the same method of juxtaposition and cross section **1.9**
used for the arabesque of the Ionic column, especially for the Pisani at
Bagnolo (II, page 47) and the Trissino at Meledo, in modern times often **1.10**
reproduced as independent decorations. Elsewhere it is merely a question
of proximity between two figures, as with the Pisani at Montagnara, the **1.11**
Zeno at Cessalto, the Cornaro, the Saraceno, the Poiana, the Valmarana,
the Lisiera, the Repeta, and so on, all examples in which the simultaneous
visibility and, I would go so far as to say, the reciprocal glorification of the
two plans and prospects are obtained. It is the illustration of the Mocenigo
sulla Brenta, which closes the second book, however, that produces the **1.12**
most beautiful page, the only figure that rests on a base formed by a few
lines of text.

Certainly the reader, should he or she desire, should be able to add to these brief notes that attempt to confirm the Palladian treatise as the most beautiful architecture volume of the Renaissance; as beautiful in its way as the narrative the *Sogno* by Polifio, illustrated with human instead of architectural shapes.

(1.) R. Pane, *Palladio*, Torino, 1948, p. 85.
(2.) I refer in particular to the erroneous interpretation of the scheme of the face of the Palazzo Chiericati (*op. cit.*, note on p. 163).
(3.) See the excellent study by M. Rosci, *Il trattato di architettura di Sebastiano Serlio,* Milano, 1927. It is to be noted that the manuscript page bears the same proportions as those of preceding books.
(4.) In my first study I had already advanced the hypothesis that two different printmakers were responsible for the prints. This seems clear if we compare the figures of the statues. See, for example, the clumsy forms in I, p. 65; II, pp. 5, 19, 21, 31, 42, 53, 74, comparing these with those that demonstrate by their elegance a more faithful adherence to the original drawings: II, pp. 9, 17, 23; III, pp. 26, 27.
(5.) For Serlio's illustrations I refer to the 1584 edition.
(6.) In my second essay I wrote: "We can only reprove Palladio for his humility in having reserved so much space for the Roman buildings and so few square centimeters for his own. And yet the book is wonderful precisely because of his economy, just as the poverty of the wood and stucco in the teatro Olimpico does not make us regret the absence of stone and marble" (p. 86). Instead, the judgment of Rosci (*op. cit.*, p. 3) concerning the *Quattro Libri* appears to me to be unacceptable, although less a real judgment than a passing comment. As frequently happens, the interest for the work in question cause the author to undervalue the works of others: "and from the *Quattro Libri* of Palladio, too proudly personal and autobiographical, implicating a total, academic renouncing of national traditions" (*op. cit.*, p. 3).

LUDWIG H. HEYDENREICH

THE VILLA: GENESIS AND DEVELOPMENT UP TO PALLADIO

The villa is one of the most important features of post-medieval architecture. A perfect example of humanistic building, it is, if not the most significant, at least one of the most characteristic "creations" of the Renaissance and is thus amongst Italy's most important contributions to world architecture.

Given the broadness of the theme, I thought it expedient to summarize the work of quite a number of scholars who, especially during the last thirty years, have done excellent work in the field.[1] I have purposely left out our illustrious predecessors from the end of the last century to the beginning of our own.[2] I would like to draw up a kind of *summa* of the contributions to research concerning the villa in an attempt to point out the "pan-Italian" aspect (the expression is from Ackerman): that is, the superregional components that contributed to the growth of the villa as *Idee und Gestalt*—form and idea—in the diverse expressions of the form in various parts of the country.

Between 1450 and 1500, a new type of secular architecture in Italy arose outside the cities: the villa as country dwelling. It had a long and complex series of prototypes, the basis of which was the ancient *topos* of the "happy country life." In the second half of the fifteenth century, responding to the spirit of the time, it grew in importance. The literary idea of the country house as a place of refuge, or *locus amoenus*, was joined with the functional aim of the building, with varying results. Thus numerous constructions arose, for the most part similar, though different in the points of detail taken from varied prototypes. Every structure was in some way determined by the "mix" of various elements proceeding from disparate circumstances. The convergence of literary and architectonic impulses made the villa the most characteristic example of a clearly humanistic architecture, in which esthetic components are just as important as ethical considerations.

The villa, therefore, rests on a literary tradition that extends from ancient times to Alberti and Sannazzaro, a tradition covering the entire Italian territory. Every province, from north to south, is represented, with

Petrarch, Boccaccio, and De Crescenzi (Bologna); Guarino (Verona); Bartolomeo Pagello (Vicenza); Leon Battista Alberti, Marsilio Ficino, Pico della Mirandola, Niccolò Machiavelli, Ermolao (Venezia); Jacopo Sannazzaro (Naples); and Paolo Giovio (Milan).[3] The villa theme is varied: next to the idealistic, moral celebration of "healthy country life" as opposed to that of the city and praise for the intellectual repose brought by villa life, there is the appreciation for the didactic and practical aspects of agriculture. These two components can be traced to Cicero, Seneca, Varron, Pliny, and Columella up to the Renaissance and reached a culmination with Alvise Cornaro's famous formula comparing farming life to that of the saints.[4] To these literary concepts was added the architectural tradition, rich in prototypes from antiquity to the fifteenth century, that inspired builders of the new villas.

Here we must distinguish between the different types of structures, from the simple farmhouse, to the fortified mansion, up to the often fanciful villas of the Romans and Arabs—not to mention the country seats of the Middle Ages, secular or religious—castles, convents, and their adjacent buildings. All these present a vast legacy of forms.[5]

The villas that went up towards the end of the fifteenth century can be divided into three main categories:

1) the *castle-villa*, which had its origins in the fortress, here lightened
2.1 and transformed into a "place of delight" (an example is the Villa Medici
Careggi or the Gonzaga palace at Revere, but there are countless examples
throughout Italy);[6]

2) the *suburban villa* and its variants up to the princely residence on
2.2 the outskirts of the city (examples: Villa Medici at Fiesole, the country
home of Cardinal Bessarione on Via Appia, the Belfiore palace [now in
2.3 ruins] at the gates of Ferrara, Poggio Reale and the "Duchessa" at Naples;[7]

3) the *villa* proper (example: Lorenzo de' Medici's villa at Poggio a
2.4 Caiano). The counterpart to the villa is the country house expanded to a
villa. I cite as example the Sforzesca near Vigevano and the Cascina near
Poggio a Caiano. I will return to these two later.[8]

2.5 As regards the prototypes that influence the rise of the Renaissance
villa, we must note that ancient monuments—at least with the great villas,
2.6 whose ruins were very visible from Sirmione to Naples—were at first completely ignored. To my knowledge, they do not even appear (a rather inter-
2.7 esting fact) among the copies of ancient monuments in architectural drawings until the beginning of the sixteenth century.[9] Not even the literary

tradition, in this preliminary stage, uses the fanciful Roman villa for material, although the small outbuilding (the *dieta* finely described by Pliny) as *locus amoenus* or place of rest is thus adopted.[10] The Belvedere of Alexander VI is also seen as a resting place inside the large complex of buildings in the Vatican.[11]

Towards the end of the fifteenth century, some motifs (such as the amphitheater and the racetrack, called the equestrian grounds) taken from the Roman villa appear in suburban residences in Naples and Mantua. These, however, were not taken directly from ancient monuments, but from descriptions found in classical texts.[12] Only in the first decade of the sixteenth century is the radical idea (which, however, appears historically valid) of "recreating" the classical Roman villa born. We will discuss this below.

The first villas of the fifteenth century derive, in terms of their structure and placement, for the most part from regional prototypes, that is from the country house. The main parts are the body of the house, widely extended, of one or two floors; the loggia, or the open, arched entry; the central room; often a tower—which can be rather low, like a dovecot—or two towers on either side. We should also consider the relationship between the building and its garden.

There are countless examples throughout Italy, with countless regional
variations, of this type of country dwelling, from farmhouse to landowner's **2.8**
home.[13] They are illustrated in many period paintings.[14]

It is hard to draw a line between the farmhouse, where agriculture is the main activity, and the country house seen as *locus amoenus*, already described by Boccaccio in the Decameron as well as by Giovanni Villani. In fact, the term *villegiatura*, meaning a place for holidays, includes the notions of both *otium* and *negotium*.[15] The union of these two ideas is essential in understanding the definition of the Renaissance villa, given the ethical significance of agriculture in humanistic thought. The expansion of agriculture had already figured among the virtues of good government (*buon governo*) for some time. The manifesto of Ercole I of Ferrara (1474), already cited by Muraro,[16] is pervaded by this idea: "Those who, with their industry and ingenuity, make every attempt to change sterile and uninhabited places into sites apt for farming and habitation, must not only be praised, but aided and encouraged with benefits, favors and immunities." A hundred years previously, in 1376, the Venetian Senate had made similar concessions.[17]

At the end of the fifteenth century, however, agriculture becomes, through the rediscovery of the teachings of Seneca, part of the education of the wise man. Accordingly, the ideal of humanism as synthesis between active and contemplative existence is realized by life in the villa.

Two buildings deserve mention here. The union of *locus amoenus* and agricultural focus is evident and appears to be the leitmotif of the places as conceived by the men who commissioned them. As such they represent the archetypes of the Renaissance villa. The first is Ludovico's Sforzesca near Vigevano, and the second is the villa at Poggio a Caiano possessed by Lorenzo de' Medici. The latter is already famous, but the Sforzesca, more austere than its cousin, is not sufficiently known. In 1463 the city government of Vigevano had granted vast tracts of land to Francesco Sforza. In 1480, Ludovico Sforza, still in power, convinced the young Duke Giangaleazzo Maria to build a villa on the land, which would serve as "noble country seat" and, at the same time, double as a model farm.

The building, finished in 1486, probably had as its architect Guglielmo da Camino, an engineer and member of the court who most likely merits further study. In any case, the villa is at the center of a piece of land measuring 20,000 *pertiche* (a *pertica* was the unit of measurement used before the adoption of the metric system in Italy; one *pertica* equals 600 square meters). Here Ludovico cultivated mulberry plants, used in the production of silk, together with grapevines and olives. The farm was turning a heavy profit in a few short years. Upon his death, the villa was left to Ludovico's wife, Beatrice d'Este; then, when she passed away, to the Dominican order of Santa Maria delle Grazie in Milan, who were the custodians of her husband's tomb.

The villa served as a summer residence for the court and was praised by chroniclers as "*amena et delectevole villa.*" One of these reports that the four buildings "are so spacious that a King might dwell there."[18] Ermolao Barbaro, Venetian ambassador to the court of Milan, wrote the praise that is still found inscribed at the entranceway, in both his original Latin and Belloncini's Italian versions: "*Ludovicus Maria divi Francisci Sforcie Mediolanensis Ducis filius divi Nepotis Tutor et Copiarum dux supremus, Planciem hanc Eterna siti Arentem, super inducta large et Ingenti sumptu aqua. Ad fertilitatem suo ingenio traduxit Villaque amenissima, a fondamentis erecta, locum sibi posterisque Comodavit. Ano salutis 1486.*"

Belloncini loosely translates thus: "I have always been a sterile, arid, uncultivated place, but now I am fertile and green due to the skillful and pious Sforza, whence I have changed my dark face and even my lowly name: whence I am now called *Sforzesca*. Ludovico loses no peace because of me: for if ever a man is born who brings peace to the world, he will have the ways of a farmer."

The Sforzesca, with its simple yet distinct style, belongs to the category of "noble country house" or "farming villa" because of its structure: four buildings with dovecot towers delimit a broad courtyard. Indeed, there is no casual resemblance between the Sforzesca and the edifice Lorenzo de' Medici had built at Poggio a Caiano during the same period. Thanks to research by Philip Foster, the plans of Lorenzo de' Medici for Poggio a Caiano are now considered to possess greater historical significance, because we can finally see how agriculture formed an intrinsic part of the
overall building project.[19] It differs from the plan for the Villa Medici at **2.9**
Fiesole (1460–70), built earlier to serve as a suburban villa used to escape city strife. Already in 1470, Lorenzo had acquired the large tract of land near Poggio a Caiano and, in the proximity of the villa itself, had built what was called a "noble farm," named the "Cascina," which is surprisingly similar to the Villa Sforzesca in Vigevano. The farm building was put up as a practical agricultural center, though with the look of a nobleman's residence well above that of a typical farm.

The villa at Poggio a Caiano bears the marks of a totally new creation and represents the metamorphosis from a rustic country home to a villa in the ancient style.[20] The simplicity of the main body of the house, its breadth, and perhaps also the open loggia in the center all belong to the tradition of the Tuscan country home. Instead, the monumental arched
base (along the lines of a Roman house, similar to the Villa dei Misteri in **2.10**
Pompeii) is from an ancient model; also similar are the regularity of the plan and the central position of the main room. Some details are also rem-
iniscent (one could almost say they are copied) of Roman prototypes, such **2.11**
as the technique of the lacunar ceiling with its barrel vaults. The pediment of the arcade seems directly inspired by Roman architecture, and, as far as I know, it is the first time that a gable from an ancient temple is used for a secular building.[21]

The humanistic concept of the villa is illustrated in the ceramic frieze **2.12**
that decorates the trabeation. The theme is a mythical-allegorical celebration of farm life, represented by the four seasons that divide the growing year, with images of grape and grain production.[22] The frieze seems a loose adaptation of the famous letter written by Marsilio Ficino to Lorenzo de'

Medici which, according to Rupprecht, might serve as the charter of the villa at Poggio a Caiano:

> *Quandoquem hodie (sicut vos astronomia docet) suspice iam, nonne vides: hodie Saturnus in coelo Phoebusque iunguntur. Hoc est Marsilii voluntas nostra sicut in coelo fit hodie, ita fieri et in terra, ut Apollinea nunc utrobique Saturniis coniungantur. O felicissimum genus humanum, si rustica Saturnii fistula Panis urbanae Phoebus citharae consonaret, semperque utriusque apud nos Dei munera iungerentur. Miscentur haec in Coelo (ut vides) apud superos hodie. Tu quoque apud homines semper miscebus in terris Vale. Vera haec ferme (ut narro) sunt magnanime Laurenti. Ito ego primum recordatus mecum ipse moerebam. Ita deinde visus est et solari, et monere me Cosmus. Ita demum Apollineum, id est, philosophicum Saturniis hominibus, id est, senioribus agricolis, tuis paravi convivium, neque id quidem absque delphica lyra. Atque colennia Cosmica qualia cumque pro tempore, pro loco, pro facultate, potuimus in Phoebea Saturnii montis academiola libentur feliciterque celebravimus. Quorsum haec? Ut oraculis Cosmianis admoniti meminerimus (si feliciter vivere volumus) caeteris quo ad fieri potest dimissis vel intermissis, Phoebum nobis simul et Saturnium Pana colendium Rustica videlicat omnia quotidie dicanda musis. Musasque vicissim ab urbanis negotiis ad Cereris agros Bacchique colles saepissime transferendas. Vale feliciter.*[23]

Towards the end of the sixteenth century the construction of villas became an overriding passion. Numerous literary sources tell us that the men who commissioned them conducted a lively exchange of opinions: for example, the correspondence between Agnolo Tovaglia, Mantuan business correspondent in Florence, and the duke Francesco Gonzaga, to whom Tovaglia sends the drawings of his villa by Leonardo da Vinci, who then made suggestions for Gonzaga's villa. Tovaglia also recommends another architect, Lorenzo da Monteacuto, who had already built numerous structures for the late Lorenzo de' Medici.[24]

Numerous documents exist, still largely ignored, which clarify the problem of artistic influences and relationships among the various regions of Italy.[25] In the early decades of the century, we witness a re-creation of

the ancient Roman villa; later in the century came the growth of a culture that grew around the villa in the region of Veneto. In addition, James Ackerman has proved that Bramante based his original plan for the courtyard of the Belvedere on the idea of renovating a Roman villa (or, more precisely, the complex that made up a Roman villa), given that its existence *in situ* was taken for granted, so that it was not "rebuilt" but merely "recreated."[26] And, thanks to Philip Foster,[27] a faithful copy of the letter that Raphael wrote to an unidentified dignitary, until now known only through various accounts by contemporaries of the famous artist, has been found,
where Raphael describes in brilliant detail his project for Villa Madama, 2.13
which was based on the imitation of a Roman model. In his description Raphael willingly adopts Roman technical terminology, such as "antechamber in the ancient mode" or "a *dieta*, thus called by the Romans." He also adopts *criptoportico*, *Xysto*, the horse ring, theater, and baths: all words that recur in the Roman writer Pliny.

Besides Bramante's and Raphael's projects for these two new large villas, the restoration of Roman villas begins at this time. One thinks of, for 2.14
example, the rebuilding of the baronial palace at Palestrina, where the
Colonna family transformed the sacred area of the temple of Fortune into 2.15
their private dwelling. Decades later, Palladio would draw on this rebuilding for his famous reconstruction.[28]

The ideal plans for the villas of Giuliano da Sangallo and Leonardo da 2.16
Vinci, carried out in the first two decades of the sixteenth century,[29] move
in the same direction, similar to the Ninfeo at Genazzano, recently redis- 2.17
covered by Christoph Frommel, which shows that it was part of a villa of
vast size.[30] 2.18

Rome furnished the thematics for the monumental villas that grew up majestically throughout Europe. After agriculture was eliminated as a component, the garden and park became essential elements of these sumptuous dwellings, and it is interesting to note how the ancient idea of "refuge" returned as part of these vast complexes in the form of small adjacent houses: the "Ermitage," the "Trianon," "Mon repos," or "Solitude": a rebirth sui generis of Pliny's *dieta*.

But let us return to the villa proper. At the threshold of the sixteenth century, we observe rapid development of the form, where the basic species evolves into very many specific types, thanks to the convergence of various local and regional components. The Villa Simonetta in Milan, begun in 1497, the Villa Bentivoglio in Bologna, the Villa Le Volte near Siena, and

the Villa Imperiale in Pesaro are only a few instances out of the countless structures that were raised throughout Italy from north to south.[31] During this second phase, that is until about 1540, the villa plays a fundamental role. Fiocco, Muraro, and Rupprecht have set out the historical, economic, and artistic factors that led to the development of the villas built during the period when Venice, with the diminishment of its sway at sea,
2.19 turned with great energy to its land possessions. With characteristic subtlety
Marco Rosci has recently shown the historical and artistic premises of the
2.20 Venice, Vicenza, and Verona regions during the fifteenth century that pre-
pare the way for the grand Palladian revolution.[32] The sampler of notable
2.21 dwellings goes on and on: to name just a few, we have Ca' Brusà, Villa
Colleoni at Thiene, Villa dei Vescovi di Falconetto in Luvigliano, Villa
2.22 Trissino at Cricoli, Villa Godi in Lonedo, and Jacopo Sansovino's Villa
Garzoni. All of these are a combination of the noble farm and the *locus*
2.23 *amoenus*. The distinctive feature is that the villa proper, the master's
dwelling that is the main part of the complex, is joined with the buildings used for agriculture—stalls, grain bins, and so on—thus determining a unitary, coherent architectonic whole.[33] We might say that agriculture itself is visibly elevated by the artistic quality of its utilitarian housing.

The great concepts that widen the ethical and humanistic notions of the villa, and that operate in men like Giangiorgio Trissino and Alvise Cornaro, are born out of the spiritual climate of celebration of agriculture. Thus the decisive impulse is given towards the artistic development of the theme that culminates with the works of Palladio.

(1.) J. S. Ackerman, *Palladio*, Hammondsworth, 1966; J. S. Ackerman, *Palladio's Villas*, Locust Valley, 1967; J. S. Ackerman, "Sources of the Renaissance Villa," in *Acts of the XXth International Congress of the History of Art*, Princeton, 1963, t. II, pp. 6 ss.; J. S. Ackerman, "The Belvedere as a Classical Villa," in *Journal of the Warburg and Courtauld Institutes*, 1957, XIV, pp. 70 ss.; U. Beseghi, *Castelli e Ville Bolognesi*, Bologna, 1964; R. Cevese, *Le Ville Vicentine*, Treviso, 1954; A. Chastel, *Art et Humanisme à Florence au temps de Laurent le Magnifique*, Paris, 1959; G. Corsi, "La villa pre-palladiana di Cusignana," in *Architettura*, 1960, n. 53, pp. 776 ss.; G. Fasolo, *Le ville del Vicentino*, Vicenza, 1929; G. Fiocco, "Alvise Cornaro," in *Bollettino C.I.S.A. A. Palladio*, Vicenza, 1963, V, pp. 33 ss.; G. Fiocco, "Le architettura di G. M. Falconetto," in *Dedalo*, 1931, p. 1230; P. Foster, "Lorenzo de' Medici's Cascina at Poggio a Caiano," in *Mit. D. Kunsthist Inst. Florenz*, 1969, XIV, pp. 47 ss.; P. Foster, "Raphael on the Villa Madama," in *Rom, Jahrb. f. Kun-*

stgeschicthe, Vienna, 1967–68, pp. 307 ss.; F. Franco, "Classicismo e funzionalità della villa palladiana 'città piccola'," in *Atti del I Congresso Nazionale di Storia dell' Architettura*,: 1936 (1941), pp. 6 ss.; F. Franco, "Piccola e grande urbanistica palladiana," in *Bollettino C.I.S.A.*, cit., 1959, I, pp. 13 ss.; C. L. Frommel, *Die Farnesian und Peruzzis architektonisches Fruhwerk*, Berlin, 1961; C. L. Frommel, "Bramante's 'Ninfeo' in Genezzano," in *Rom Jahrb. f. Kunstgeschicthe*, 1969, XII, pp. 137, ss.; G. Lorenzoni, *Lorenzo da Bologna*, Venezia, 1963; T. Magnuson, Studies in Roman Quattrocento Architecture, in *Figura*, 1958, IX; G. Mansuelli, *Le ville nel mondo romano*, Milano, 1958; G. Masson, "Palladian Villas as rural centers," in *The Architectural Review*, 1955, pp. 137 ss.; G. Mazzotti, *Ville Venete*, Roma, 1967; M. Muraro, *Treasures of Venice*, Geneva, 1963; M. Muraro, *Civiltà delle ville venete*, Rotaprint, 1964; B. Nice, *La casa rurale nella Venezia Giulia*, Florence, 1940; R. Pane, *Architettura del Rinascimento in Napoli*, Napoli, 1937; R. Pane, "Tipi di architettura rustica in Napoli e nei Campi Flegrei," in *Architettura*, 1927–28, VII, pp. 529 ss.; R. Pane, *Andrea Palladio*, Torino, 1961; L. Puppi, "La Villa Garzoni," in *Prospettiva*, 1961, XI, 24, pp. 51 ss.; M. Rosci, *Il Trattato di Architettura di Sebastiano Serlio*, Milano, 1966; M. Rosci, "Forme e funzioni delle ville venete prepalladiane," in *L'arte*, 1968, 2, pp. 27 ss.; B. Rupprecht, "Die Villa Garzoni des jacopo Sansovino," in *Mitt. Kunsthist. Inst. Florenz*, 1963, XI, pp. 4 ss.; B. Rupprecht, "Ville Venete del '400 e del primo '500," in *Bollettino C.I.S.A.*, cit., 1964, VI, p. II, pp. 239 ss.; B. Rupprecht, "Villa, Zur Geschichte einer Ideals," in *Probleme der Kunstwissenschaft*, II, Berlin, 1966, pp. 120 ss.; G. Sandri, "Problemi di Storia Veronese, Origini della villegiatura," in *Bollettino Soc. Lett. Verona*, 1931, pp. 3 ss.; G. Silvestri, *La Valpolicella*, Verona, 1950; P. Tomei, *L'architettura a Roma nel Quattrocento*, Roma, 1942; R. Wittkower, *Architectural Principles in the Age of Humanism*, London, 1952; G. G. Zorzi, *Le ville e I teatri di Andrea Palladio*, Vicenza, 1969.

(2.) J. Burckhardt, *Geschichte der Renaissance in Italien*, Stuttgart, 1891, pp. 116–18; C. Stegmann-H. v. Geymueller, *Baukunst der Renaissance in Italien*, Munich, 1908, X; B. Patzak, *Palast und Villa in Toskana*, Leipzig, 1912–13, I, 1/2; K. Swoboda, *Romische und romanische Palaste*, Vienna, 1924; E. Lovarini, *Le ville edificate da A. Cornaro*, Rome, 1899.

(3.) Cfr. B. Rupprecht, "Villa, Zur," cit.; M. Muraro, *Civiltà*, cit.

(4.) M. Muraro, *Civiltà*, cit.

(5.) B. Patzak, *Palast und*, cit., I, p. 1 passim, and M. Muraro, *Civiltà*, cit., pp. 3 ss.

(6.) Villa Medici—Careggi: O. Morisani, *Michelangelo architetto*, Turin, 1951, pp. 40 ss. Palazzo villa Gonzaga: E. Marani, in "Mantova," *Le Arti*, 1961, pp. 70 ss.

(7.) Villa Medici in Fiesole: C. L. Frommel, *Die Farnesian*, cit., pp. 85 ss.; O. Morisani, *Michelangelo architetto*, cit., p. 72; Casa Bessarione: P. Tomei, *op. cit.*, p. 31; Villa Belfiore (Ferrara): G. Gruyer, *L'Art Ferrarais à l'époque des Princes d'Este*, Paris, 1897, I, p. 468; Poggio Reale e la "Duchessa" in Naples: R. Pane, *op. cit.*, pp. 15 ss.; C. L. Frommel, *Farnesina*, cit., pp. 90 ss.

(8.) Cfr. note 17 and 19.

(9.) No studies of ancient villas are found among the drawings of Francesco by Giorgio Martini, Giuliano da Sangallo, or in the Cronaca, nor in the *codice Escorialense* or similar notebooks.
(10.) Cfr. L. H. Heydenreich, "Federico da Montefeltre as a Building Patron," in *Studies in Renaissance and Baroque Art presented to Anthony Blunt*, London, 1967, pp. 1 ss.
(11.) Cfr. D. Redis de Campos, "Il Belvedere d'Innocenzo VIII in Vaticano," in *Triplice omaggio a SS. Pio XII*, Vatican City, 1958, pp. 289 ss.
(12.) Cfr. E. Marani, in "Mantova," cit., pp. 204 ss.; R. Pane, *op. cit.*, p. 25; A. Colombo, "Palazzo e Giardino di Poggio Reale," in *Napoli Nobilissima*, 1892, I, pp. 117 ss., 136 ss., 166 ss.
(13.) Cfr. C. Stegmann-H. v. Geymueller, *op. cit.*; J. S. Ackerman, "Sources," cit.; U. Beseghi, *op. cit.*; M. Rosci, "Forme e funzioni," cit.; B. Rupprecht, "Ville Venete," cit., p. 3.
(14.) Cfr. B. Patzak, *op cit.*, I, pp. 126–29. the two rural buildings are also very beautiful on the "Buon Governo" fresco by Lorenzetti in Siena: a castle-villa and a farmhouse (with open loggia). Cfr. *I grandi decoratori: Ambrogio Lorenzetti. La sala della Pace*, Fabbri-Skira, 1968, pp. 34, 38–40.
(15.) B. Rupprecht, "Ville Venete," cit., p. 214; G. Sandri, *op. cit.*, p. 3.
(16.) M. Muraro, *Civiltà*, cit., p. 17
(17.) F. Malaguzzi-Valeri, *La Corte di Ludovico il Moro*, Milan, 1913, I, p. 664.
(18.) F. Malaguzzi-Valeri, *op. cit.*, p. 667.
(19.) P. Foster, "Lorenzo de' Medici's Cascina," cit.
(20.) R. Marchini, *Giuliano da Sangallo*, Florence, 1943, pp. 16, 85. Phillip Foster is preparing a large monograph on Poggio a Caiano.
(21.) The vault is reproduced in P. Sanpaolesi, *Brunelleschi*, Milan, 1962, tables XIII and XIV (color). Cfr. also P. Sanpaolesi, "Il Palazzo Scala," in *Toskanische Studien*. Festschrift fur L. H. Heydenreich, Munich, 1963, p. 279.
(22.) Cfr. A. Chastel, *op. cit.*, pp. 148 ss.
(23.) B. Rupprecht, "Ville Venete," cit., p. 234.
(24.) C. Pedretti, *A Chronology of Leonardo da Vinci's Architectural Studies After 1500*, Geneva, 1962, p. 25. See also the review of the "Raccolta Vinciniana," 1962, XX, pp. 410 ss.
(25.) There was an equestrian habit amongst the men who commissioned these homes—Medici, Sforza, Gonzaga, Aragonesi, Montefeltre, and many others. These should be kept in mind as regards various architectural enterprises. These men asked for and offered advice to their architects. Concerning such relationships there is still much work to be done.
(26.) J. S. Ackerman, "The Belvedere," cit.
(27.) P. Foster, "Raphael," cit.; C. L. Frommel, "La villa Madama e la tipologia della villa romana nel rinascimento," in *Bollettino del Centro Internazionale di Studi d'Architettura, Andrea Palladio*, 1969, XI.
(28.) L. H. Heydenreich, "Der Palazzo Baronale der Colonna in Palestrina," in

Walter Friedländer zum 90. Geburtstag, Berlin, 1965, pp. 85 ss.
(29.) G. G. Zorzi, *I disegni delle Antichità di Andrea Palladio*, Venezia, 1959, pp. 200–204.
(30.) R. Marchini, *Giuliano da Sangallo*, cit., pp. 88, 89, 101; C. Pedrotti, *A Chronology*, cit., pp. 112 ss.
(31.) Cfr. C. L. Frommel, "Bramante's 'Ninfeo,'" cit.
(32.) Villa Simonetta in Milan: P. Mezzanotte, B. P. Bascapè, *Milano nell'arte e nella storia*, Milano, 1948, p. 771; Villa Bentivoglia, called "La Viola" (Bologna): G. Zucchini, *Edifici di Bologna*, Roma, 1931, p. 148; G. Zucchini, "Una palazzina Bentivolesca colpita e ricostruita," in *Atti del v Congresso Nazionale dell' Architettura*, 1948, Firenze, 1957, pp. 649 ss.; Villa Delle Volte (Siena): B. Patzak, *op. cit.*, I, p. 143; C. L. Frommel, *Die Farnesian*, cit., pp. 106 ss.; Villa Imperiale di Pesaro: B. Patzak, *Die Ville Imperiale a Pesaro*, Leipzig, 1908.
(33.) M. Rosci, *Forme e funzioni*, cit.

MARIO ZOCCONI

THE COURTYARDS OF PALLADIAN BUILDINGS

A comparison of the forms, functions, and structures of the courtyard in the planning of Palladian townhouses and villas is a typological rather than a critical analysis. Therefore, with the present article, we simply wish to verify measurements and functional variants and to see how the works came into being, were developed, and were reused in other works by Palladio, always keeping in mind the limited scope of our research.

Palladio thought of the courtyard as we do today, that is, as an open space delimited by buildings, looked upon by the windows of the inside rooms. Courtyards generally have four sides, which are usually, but not always, walls of buildings, particularly in "townhouses." In country villas, apart from rare exceptions, the buildings are on three sides, and the courtyard is closed by simple walls or by hedges.

We are basing our observations on a reading of the *Quattro Libri* for several reasons: either because more modern texts are rarely as clear, or because the buildings were not finished, or because changes were made to the structures later on.[1] Yet the indications in the *Quattro Libri*, especially for villa courtyards, are not always precise, because the engravings sometimes do not show complete delimitations. Often the courtyards are not even shown but are discussed in the text, as is the case with Villa Valmarana: "one [courtyard] in the front for the master's use, and another for threshing the grain" (Book II, page 59). Elsewhere the open spaces, partially closed in by buildings, appear to be courtyards (in the rather schematic engravings), but the author labels them "gardens," even when the interior spaces do not appear destined for that activity.

Palladio places courtyards with the main parts of the house, writing that the utmost care should be taken with these as well as other elements, "so that the house will be comfortable for the family" (Book II, page 3). However, Wittkower has shown that in practice the courtyard for Palladio is "the most important part of the house."[2] And so it seems from the composition, function, and architectonic decoration. As for the composition and decoration of the courtyard walls, note that in some of Palladio's drawings, the external views are placed next to those of the inner courtyard walls, as in the London drawings.[3] This placement occurs with Palazzo Valmarana and Palazzo Iseppo da Porto in Vicenza; and according to Decio Gioseffi, the façade of Palazzo Valmarana comes from the elevation (across the courtyard) of Palazzo Iseppo da Porto.[4]

The importance that Palladio attaches to the courtyard is clear also from the second book of his treatise. Many figures present clear outlines of the courtyards, not only in the plans, but also the elevations (which are clearly sectional views). When the figures are detailed, views of courtyards are placed beside those of the façade, as with the Palazzo Iseppo da Porto (Book II, pages 8, 10), and Thiene (Book II, pages 13–14). In the illustrations of Palazzo Dalla Torre in Verona (Book II, page 11) and of the Della Carità convent in Venice (Book II, pages 30, 32), only courtyard views are found, without any external views, since with these buildings, which were inserted into a preexisting urban context, the outside façades counted less than the inside surfaces. This importance is reflected in the illustrations. The same goes for several illustrations of villas, in particular Thiene (Book II, page 64) and Sarego in Santa Sofia (Book II, page 67), **3.1**
where we see only the sections of the main courtyards. Today we can see only a small part of the outside plan of Palazzo Thiene, but it gives us an idea of the potential grandiosity and magnificence of the complex that might have developed around the courtyard following the Palladian conception of "small city" (*città piccola*) described in Book II on page 46. In Palazzo Sarego, the existing parts of the courtyard clearly show the central role Palladio intended for the space.

The *Quattro Libri* also reveal how Palladio studied the courtyards of Roman buildings and include mention of Vitruvius's observations on their proportions. The architect also studies Greek and Roman squares, which he sees, in the above-mentioned passage of the *Quattro Libri*, as the courtyards of that larger house that is the city. Not only does Palladio show the structures and proportions of these ancient public spaces, but he also supplies illustrations that give us a critical and historical reading superior to any other commentator of Vitruvius.

In the treatise called "Dell'Atrio Toscano" ("On Tuscan Atria," Book II, page 24), Palladio indicates the *peristilio* or peristyle as "a courtyard **3.2**
with porticoes surrounding it" and gives the Vitruvian rules for its proportions: "one third longer than it is wide." In the two figures illustrating the house called degli Antichi (Book II, pages 25, 26) two "gardens" on the sides of the atrium are indicated with a portico on one side that wraps

around the corners in the same way as in the courtyard of Palazzo Barbaran da Porto. Another courtyard, at the rear of the house, has porticoes on three sides and is open on the fourth. In the axonometric projection we have tried to create a graphic interpretation of the text of Vitruvius describing the plan and a section of the Casa degli Antichi, with a detail in Vitruvius of the atrium area. Considering that the two plates present diverse solutions, we have used the larger scale illustration that is clearly the result of more extensive study.

For the rear of the house, the details of which appear only as part of the group of illustrations, we have come up with one possible solution. The section of this part is difficult to interpret and almost certainly erroneous. In fact, the plan is not continuous, but is deflected onto the room with four columns, eliminating the illustration of the courtyard with porticoes on three sides, and the covering has been moved onto this room erroneously, leaving a part of the portico of the main courtyard uncovered. The obscurity of Palladio's last sentence in the text makes interpretation of his illustration even more difficult: "There is no covering over the passages, but here are balconies: and depending on the site one could build more or less than I have drawn here, also taking into consideration the intended use and the wishes of the inhabitants." We must consider here that by "passages" Palladio meant the covered passages around the last courtyard. Therefore this would have only one order of columns and a terrace as cover, what he calls "balconies." In fact, only this part of the house could be lengthened according to the use intended.

In writing the "Dell'Atrio Testugginato e della Casa Privata degli Antichi Romani" (Book II, page 33), Palladio refers only to the "peristyle" "which has porticoes which are as wide as the lengths of the columns." However, in the figures on pages 34–35 he indicates two courtyards, open on the atrium side, with porticoes on one side only, and another two spaces next to the "basilica" with columns on two contiguous sides.

3.3 In the "Case Private de' Greci" (Book II, page 43), there are more courtyards: the first, which, he writes, "has porticoes on three sides," onto which the services areas give, while on the fourth side an ample entrance opens onto rooms for the family; and a second, larger courtyard in a more extensive building, with porticoes of equal height surrounding it. The author also indicates a variant of the latter courtyard: the so-called "Rhodiaco" court, with a higher portico on one side, and he illustrates it with a plate in Book II, page 44, where the high portico is projected on the background and the low porticoes are sectioned, with a floor above with rooms.[5] Other courtyards can be seen in the same plate, with loggia on one side, as part of adjacent guest houses.

Open spaces with colonnades on all four sides or on two contiguous sides are illustrated in the plate labeled "Delle Piazza de i Greci" in chapter 17 of the third book, or in the section "Delle Piazza de' Latini," in chapter 18 of the same book. However, these conceptions, although they 3.4
are linked to the peristyle of the ancient house, obviously are of different sizes corresponding to their diverse, though analogous, functions. Another courtyard with arcades is found in the print for the treasury for the "Vitruvius" of Barbaro.[6]

Palladio tends to cling to these Vitruvian types of courtyards both in his drawings and in actual building.[7] Above all, we see that Palladio retains the rectangular forms of the courtyards of the ancient structures for his own, although the need to adjust according to the site (Book II, page 71) might not always allow this. In general, the irregularities of the sites affect some rooms or small secondary courtyards, the main courtyard remaining aligned with the entrance and four sided with right angles, as in the "Venetian site" (Book II, page 72) in the Capra house of Vicenza and in the finished parts of Palazzo Barbaran da Porto and Palazzo Valmarana. The *sito piramidale* or pyramidal site in Book II, page 71, where the courtyard is an irregular pentagon with three consecutive right angles, is an exception. An example of a courtyard that is not four-sided is that of Palazzo Breganze in Vicenza, which has a side in a semicircle, although we do not know whether the curve was already in Palladio's plans or if it is due to a variant of Vincenzo Scamozzi. The courtyards of some villas also have semicircular sides, but some are to be considered exedras rather than courtyards. Palladio wrote of the project for Villa Mocenigo sulla Brenta that the 3.5
exedras "tend toward the circumference like arms, appearing to welcome those who approach the house."

We have seen that in the houses of antiquity, all the courtyards have arcades with columns, and that these arcades can be arranged in different ways: on all four sides, on three sides only, on one side and a part of the two contiguous sides, on two opposing sides, or else on only one. Palladio, in the plates of his treatise, supplies us with all of these, but he adds courtyards where, instead of columns and architraves, there are pilasters and arches, or courtyards with columns on all four sides, but with one side partially occupied by a staircase, or even courtyards without arcades, but with a loggia in only the central part of one side.

It is odd that one of the first courtyards he presents in his treatise, that
3.6 of Palazzo Chiericati (Book II, page 6), is merely a modest service area, despite the vast loggia that gives upon it. It is of a narrow rectangular form, partly taken up, on two corners, by two spiral staircases. Its width is barely eighteen paces. Apparently the vast loggia mentioned above is meant to be as significant as the courtyards in other buildings. The limited available land, occupied for the most part by the external loggia, must have been the reason for the plan. The building was enlarged in later years and the courtyard expanded. This design can be linked to those without arcades but with a loggia as part of the main body of the building, like the one in Palladio's treatise in a house for a *sito piramidale*. The internal gardens of Palazzo
3.7 Antonini in Udine (Book II, page 5) and of Villa Pisani (Book II, page 52), can be considered courtyards of the type just mentioned, because of the loggias that look out on them.

The courtyards of Palazzo Iseppo da Porto, now called Festa, the inside court of Villa Sarego, and that of the sketch for Palazzo Trissino found in Book II, page 74, are genuine peristyles, but unfortunately none of these were built according to Palladio's conception. The courtyards of Palazzo Thiene and of the Cloister della Carità in Venice are rectangular with porticoes on all sides, but unlike those mentioned above, they do not have columns, but pilasters joining arches. Therefore they cannot be compared to ancient peristyles, though they serve the same function and have the same characteristics.[8] These courtyards also are not completely finished, but the single side that is completed is enough to give us an idea of Palladio's overall plan.

The courtyards that appear in the engravings for Palazzo Angarano in Vicenza and Villa Mocenigo sulla Brenta also have porticoes on four sides (Book II, page 75), but both have one side partially closed by the wall in front of the stairway. The first, in fact, has two contiguous courtyards separated by the staircase, the one accessible from the atrium being smaller, with pilasters on only three sides.

It is hard to know what the courtyard of Palazzo Barbaran da Porto
3.8 was supposed to be like, since the figure in Book II, page 22, is of a courtyard with porticoes on only one side, on an axis with the atrium. In addition, the text tells us that it was not to be modified, but merely closed on one side by another structure with "rooms for the kitchen, for serving women, and other facilities," thus conserving "the same order in both

parts." The structure we have, however, presents an arcade with two orders of columns along the whole side, at the left of the entry, which turns again with two intercolumniations, joining the wall that closes the atrium at the ground floor and the main room of the floor above. This solution is related in part to the two courtyards at the sides of the basilica of the private house of the ancient Romans. Clearly this courtyard does not correspond to the one Palladio describes, and the notable dissymmetry of the internal façade as regards the atrium would have required a portico perfectly symmetrical to the one built, which, however, would have occupied all of the available space, without leaving room for the "stalls and servants' quarters." These considerations might lead us to think of an enlargement unsupervised by Palladio, but the actual execution would seem to indicate his mastery.[9]

In the engraving for Palazzo Valmarana we see courtyards with porticoes only on two opposite sides (Book II, page 16) and that of the idea for a "site in the Veneto region." The finished section of the first building, which includes the main body on the road with internal portico and a lateral wing on the courtyard, does not give us a precise idea of what Palladio's conception might have been. The existing portico, very high and deep, was not perfectly echoed in the one opposite, which is as deep but slightly less ample. The notable height of the structures that face into the courtyard and the heavy overhanging of the balcony, held up by robust brackets, which in the plan was supposed to run along all sides, would have furnished a dimly lit space, especially if the internal structure had been the height of the one facing the road. This convinces us that the height of the internal part was supposed to be limited to the ground floor.

The engraving for the palazzo for Giulio Capra in Vicenza presents us 3.9
with a courtyard with a portico on one side, like that of Palazzo Bonin Longare. However, while the first has pilasters that suppose a plan with arches and inset columns, as in the Cloister of the Carità, the second has a plan that
reflects the drawing of the detail for the Piazza dei Greci (Book III, page 3.10
34), if we are to consider it as conceived with the procedure indicated by Gioseffi, who has been mentioned in connection with Palazzo Valmarana.

The project for Palazzo Dalla Torre in Verona presents a peculiar form for a city dwelling, with two entries and two courtyards separated by an "open room." The courtyards, taken individually, are related to those with a loggia on one side only, but in this case the covered space is not placed on the side of the entry, but opposite it. The courtyards are labeled as measuring thirty-four by fifty feet and are therefore related to the peristyle indicated in the treatise some pages later. It should be noted that while in the drawing of the plan the two courtyards are the same, in the section, one has two orders of columns or pillars, and the other has only the cornice with brackets that form the balcony. This difference can be explained by the fact that the site "has the main road on one of the lesser sides," so that the courtyard with columns would be the receiving one. The difference leads us to believe that the dissimilarity in the orders of columns, in the figure of the Tuscan atrium, cannot be attributed to an error on the part of the engraver, but is desired by the author in order to let us know that structural or decorative symmetries must not always perfectly correspond to planimetric symmetries.

As we have seen, the unfinished courtyard of Palazzo Porto Breganze,
3.11 which Bertotti presents with his handsome engravings, is completely
remarkable.[10] The work, which Vincenzo Scamozzi claims to have finished (Pane), was certainly begun after the publication of Palladio's treatise and was most likely built based on drawings made in his later years. The semicircular form may be compared to the exedra-shaped porticoes of the villas or the portico above the stairs of the Teatro Olimpico.

In the section "Case di Ville," the courtyards, when they are not conceived as peristyles, have porticoes on three sides, with the fourth closed by a wall, as in Villa Repeta a Campiglia (Book II, page 61), where a part of the wall is curved, and in Villa Thiene di Quinto, with its large, rustic courtyard, or else in Villa Sarengo, with the entrance court (which, however, is open on one side). In other courtyards of this form, the arcade of the main side is divided at the center from the body of the building or by an access stairway, as in Villa Zeno a Cessalto (Book II, page 49), Saraceno a Finale (Book II, page 56), Ragona a Ghizzole (Book II, page 57), or Villa Angarano (Book II, page 63).

To tell the truth, we cannot be sure that the courtyards of Villa Sara-
3.12 ceno or Villa Ragona, as well as that of Quinto Vicentino, have arcades on
only three sides, insofar as the relative engravings lack the fourth side com-
3.13 pletely. Only the illustration of Villa Pisani di Bagnolo (Book II, page 47)
has a courtyard closed in by structures with arcades on all four sides. A staircase and a pronaos divide one main side of the courtyard. None of these were ever in fact built, and the actual façade, given its real size compared to the dimensions reported in the engraving, could not have included such a large pronaos.

We have already noted the courtyards with curved arcades. The pur-

pose for these seems to exclude any utility except for cover from the elements, while rectangular courtyards may be used merely for farm work or for show. In fact, spaces used for farm work are never enclosed with the curved sort of courtyard. The curved porticoes of Villa Badoer di Fratta Polesine (Book II, page 48) or Villa Thiene at Cicogna (Book II, page 63) **3.14**
probably serve general and esthetic purposes, while the exedra portico in the rear of Villa Sarego is simply an object that delimits space.

In Book II we find engravings that illustrate other types of courtyards found in ancient homes. These include courtyards with longer arcades on opposite sides, as in the space behind the façade of Villa Godi di Lonedo (Book II, page 65), in the lateral courtyards of Villa Thiene di Quinto, and at the rear of Villa Mocenigo at Marocco (Book II, page 54). We also find one with arcades on two contiguous sides bordering the main building of Villa Poiana (Book II, page 58). Courts with only one arcade can be made out in the prints of Villa Barbaro at Maser (Book II, page 51) and Villa **3.15**
Emo at Fanzolo (Book II, page 55). In these villas, however, we do not really see true courtyards, but rather the arrangement of large garden spaces, as seen today. At the rear of Villa Barbaro we find the only example of a courtyard without any arcade; the "ornament" consists of the part "where in the hillock against the house a fountain with a multitude of decorations in stucco and paint is placed."[11]

As we have already seen, Palladio brings the Vitruvian rules of proportion regarding courtyards and their parts into his treatise.[12] A courtyard must be "a third longer than it is wide" (Book II, page 24), or else "a square and a half" (*un quadro e mezo*, page 27). The Greeks made their squares "in square form," and the Romans "divided the length into three parts, and made the width two." The porticoes were "as wide as the columns were tall" (Book II, page 39; Book III, pages 32, 35), but in the gardens the portico should be as wide as the intercolumns. Checking the relationship between the sides, the width, and the height of the porticoes, in both the actual courtyards and those illustrated in the treatise, we may conclude that Palladio rarely followed this rule, not only in the city dwellings, but also in the villas, where space was almost never limited.

In the print for Palazzo Iseppo da Porto, the courtyard has nearly a square shape: the sides have a ratio of 1:1.05. The arcade is 10 feet wide in the overall view, but is measured 7.25 in the detailed illustration, and its width is much smaller than the height of the walls supporting the "floor of the loggia above," being almost equal to the height of the intercolumns.

The courtyard in the engraving of Palazzo Thiene bears measurements that make it perfectly square: each side is 74 feet, or 25.71 meters. One side of the actual courtyard, instead, measures 20.37, with another 22.39. The span of the arches is different on the two sides (2.55 and 2.70 meters). It is known that the sides of the courtyard were not built according to the complete plan and should measure 25.45 and 26.70 meters, respectively, therefore giving the space a 1:1.05 ratio, as seen in Palazzo da Porto. The width of the arcades is also significantly inferior to their height. In the cloisters of the Carità, the measurements reported in the *Quattro Libri* present a 1:1.26 ratio, which approaches the Vitruvian norm. The space as it has come down to us, instead, is larger, because demolition and modifications have altered the previous form.[13] Here also the width of the arcade is much less than the height, being about half.

The courtyard in the illustration of Palazzo Barbaran da Porto in Vicenza follows Vitruvius, being 25 feet wide and 33 long. However, we have already seen how this courtyard was substantially altered from the very beginning of its construction. In the actual building, it does not even have orthogonal sides, but the ratio of the sides is still Vitruvian. The portico is about 20 feet high, with a width of 6.3. In the print of Palazzo Angarano, the sides of the courtyard with pilasters have a ration of 1:1.7, therefore of more than a square and a half; and the other, with two orders, is square. Villa Mocenigo sulla Brenta has an internal courtyard with a 1:1.27 ratio, nearly a square and a half, the width of the arcade being slightly less than its height: "less than a column diameter." In Palazzo Valmarana the courtyard is perfectly square, and the measurements of the print are nearly the same as the actual space. The loggia is 6.9 meters deep and 7.33 meters high.

The planimetric form and the ratio of the sides of the courtyards do not always correspond to Vitruvius's rules that Palladio includes in his treatise, but it would be interesting to check the ratio between the width of the courtyards and the height of the delimiting structures. Palladio is silent concerning this ratio, at least as regards courtyards, but in many passages he repeats the proportions for the rooms and atria: "in the solarium, the height from floor to roof will be equal to their width" (Book I, page 53). Of the testudo style atrium he writes: "the height up to just under the beams is equal to the width" (Book II, page 33). These are evidently rules that Palladio tries to follow for courtyards also; in fact, in the figures for "Dell'Atrio Toscano," with ancient houses, in that for "Dell'Atrio

Corinthio" (Book II, page 29), with the cloisters of the Carità, as well as the images of Palazzo Iseppo da Porto and Palazzo Thiene, the height is in fact equal to the width. The same proportions, more or less, are found also in the courtyard of Palazzo Valmarana, the main courtyard of Palazzo Anagarano, and the interior space of Villa Mocenigo sulla Brenta.

At Palazzo Trissino in Vicenza, the height of the courtyard is the same as that of the external façade; it is also equal to the average length and width of the courtyard. In Palazzo Barbaran da Porto, if the dimensions of the courtyard were developed completely as regards the longitudinal axis, the width would be equal to the average of the height of the main building and the wing with arcade. In Villa Thiene the height of the high structures corresponds to the width of the courtyard, while the smaller structures are one-third of that height.

It is interesting to note that in all these courtyards, as in others Palladio designed, the width in general, compared to the height, is larger than the limits imposed by modern building norms, and therefore the ratio between the courtyard surface and that of the walls that enclose it is also larger. Thus we may affirm that Palladio took care to respect not only rules of esthetics, but also health. In fact, smaller courtyards, including those contained in the *Quattro Libri*, have an area that is one-fifth larger than the height of the walls, the minimum prescribed by modern building codes, while up until a few years ago the codes permitted one-tenth or one-twelfth.

The courtyard of the palazzo for Count G. B. Dalla Torre in Verona has a surface area over a fourth of that of the walls. That of Palazzo Valmarana is a little under one-quarter, if the interior building structure is assumed to be limited in height, and measures 1:4.4, with the entire perimeter equal to the height of the façade. The exception is found in the figure for Palazzo Chiericati, where the courtyard is very narrow but has a surface area of 15 feet, subtracting the area of two spiral stairways, and is one-sixth the size of the surrounding walls, supposing that the wall enclosure was planned to be very high.

(1.) The references to *I Quattro Libri dell' Architettura*, Venice, 1570, are indicated in parentheses with the Roman numeral the book, and Arabic numerals for pages.
(2.) R. Wittkower, *Principi architettonici nell'età dell'Umanesimo*, Italian translated, Turin, 1964, p. 80.
(3.) Cfr. the London drawings, R.I.B.A. XVII, 4r and XVII, 3.
(4.) D. Gioseffi, "Il disegno come fase progetturale dell'attività palladiana," in *Bollettino del Centro Internazionale di Studi di Architettura A. Palladio*, Vicenza, 1972, XIV, p. 61.
(5.) Doubtlessly Palladio did not study the architectonic problems of this courtyard in detail, so named "*forse per esser venuta l'inventione da Rhodi.*" This is because, in the engraving, the columns of the high arcade are clearly indicated in elevation, as well as those of the low arcades, all Corinthian. But in the plan, both the diameters and the intercolumns are the same, therefore with a notable discordance with the rules of proportion in Book I.
(6.) The *Dieci Libri dell'Architettura tradutti et commentati da monsignor Barbaro eletto Patriarca d'Aquileggia. In Vinegia per Francesco Marcolini*—MDLVI, chap. II, p. 167.
(7.) We could also consider atria to be courtyards, assuming that the words *vesitibula, alta atria*, and *casa aedium* mean the same thing, words that appear in Vitruvius and that have generated one of the many problems in interpreting his book. (See *L'Architettura di M. Vitruvio Pollione colla traduzione italiana e commento del marchese Berardo Galiani, ecc.*, Naples, 1758, p. 230, note 3, for these problems of interpretation. However, for Palladio the "*casa aedium*" of Vitruvius are the atria and not the courtyards, thus we also consider these spaces as amongst the closed ones, even if they are sometimes partially open at the center.
(8.) Vitruvius, VI, 4, refers only to columns and intercolumns: "*Peristyliorum intercolumnia ne minus trium, ne plus quator columnarum crassitudine inter se distent*" (B. Galiani, *op. cit.*, p. 232). Palladio's drawings for Barbaro and in the *Quattro Libri* present only peristyles as columns. The courtyard of the convent of the Carità is indicated by Palladio as "*Inclaustro*" (Book II, p. 29), but E. Bassi in his volume on this building (*Il convento della Carità*, Vincenza, 1971) indicates it also as peristyle (color figure *C* in appendix). In all other buildings these spaces are never indicated as peristyles.
(9.) R. Pane, *Andrea Palladio*, Turin, 1961, p. 356: "The loggias are built so as to stand comparison with the best buildings of the time. In fact, here the completeness of the detail is rendered more evident from the current state of abandonment, because, large parts of the stucco having fallen from the trabeation, here and there the fine alteration between shaped stone and brick is clearly recognizable, bearing witness to Palladio's mastery as builder. There is also a refined tonal sense in the structure with Ionic capitals whose smooth surface is left grandine to give contrast to the smooth surface of the shafts."
(10.) O. Bertotti Scamozzi, *Le fabbriche e i disegni di Andrea Palladio*, Vicenza, 1776, I, fig. XXXII, XXXIII, XXXIV.

(11.) The rear courtyard of Villa Godi at Lonedo is planimetrically similar to that of Villa Maser, but because of the sloping terrain, the curved part does not penetrate the hill, but advances, supported by a high wall, towards the gardens below, the views of which make up the "ornament" of this courtyard. Palladio foresaw this arrangement also for the rear of Villa Maser, but with less abrupt changes of level, due to the more gentle sloping of the terrain.

(12.) Vitruvius, VI, 4: "*Peristylia autem in trasverso tertia parte longiora sint quam introrsus*" (B. Galiani, *op. cit.*).

(13.) Cfr. E. Bassi, *op. cit.*

FAULTS AND ABUSES OF LORD BURLINGTON'S PUBLICATION OF PALLADIO'S DRAWINGS OF CLASSICAL ANTIQUITY

The drawings of the Roman baths published by Richard, Lord Burlington in 1730 under the title *Buildings of Classical Antiquity Drawn by Andrea Palladio, of Vicenza*, have been thought until now to be faithful reproductions of the sketches that Burlington acquired during his travels in Italy in 1719. The volume, richly illustrated by the engraver Fourdrinier, bore a preface entitled "to the discerning reader," saying that the drawings depicted only some of the Roman baths and that Burlington had found them "bound together as if set for publication," so that he had only to print them "in the same form and dimension in which I found them, without any changes." However, we think it necessary to place scholars on guard concerning these claims with a few simple caveats.

To this end, let us remember that the French architect Charles Chameron[1] was influenced by the volume put out by Burlington, as was Ottavio Bertotti Scamozzi of Vicenza,[2] and that they circulated the published drawings. Like Burlington, however, neither of these two men reproduced the designs exactly.

Although Chameron bases his treatise, the *Description des Bains des Romains enrichie des plans de Palladio*, on Burlington, he adds "a good number of figures, sketches and other pieces from antiquity" (of which only a few deal with the Roman baths) in order to complete and produce a more impressive work. He also, thereby, makes it a work of his own, and not merely a facile copying.

Bertotti, for his part, intended to reprint only the drawings of the baths done by Palladio, or identified as such by Burlington, but he added a few notes and some erroneous identifications and marked the plans of the baths with lines to point out where the objects in the drawings had been rendered as cross sections. He also informed the reader that "In the plans, some of the labels have been turned around to show that the cross-sections should be seen from that side." He then concluded, "I think it necessary to add an explanation of the headings which were given to those descriptions by the honorable Chameron."

Bertotti added, however, that he could not be the "guarantor" for Chameron's statements concerning "his methods for some of the parts," thus demonstrating his lack of firsthand knowledge of the monuments depicted.

We see thus how both Chameron and Bertotti added something of their own to the drawings published by Burlington. In order to proceed accurately we must examine Burlington's volume to see whether he faithfully reproduced Palladio's drawings or whether there are faults or abuses. It is certain that the actual monuments depicted and details thereof may be identified with the sole aid of Palladio's original drawings. It is also certain that Burlington did not publish the identifications in Palladio's hand and that he left out many measurements and numbers found in the originals, reproduced in my volume *I designi delle Antichità di Andrea Palladio.*[3]

We should note, first of all, that Burlington did not reproduce the plan of the Baths of Agrippa, published instead by Bertotti Scamozzi, who followed the original drawing in the Vicenza Museum. Neither did he reproduce any of the preparatory sketches (which can be seen in my volume), which he possessed but failed to identify, of the plan itself. As far as the elevations of the baths go, Burlington reproduced neither the measurements that figure in the original (also in my volume) nor the shading, thus leaving out information that might have shed some light on the devices used by Palladio in his reproductions and reconstructions of the monuments from classical antiquity. The same can be said regarding the drawings of the baths of Constantine, Titus, Trajan, Nero, Caracalla, and Diocletian. To sum up, we can safely say that all of Burlington's reproductions contain notable faults and inadequacies, such that they can be considered neither accurate nor particularly reliable, insofar as they neither demonstrate the way in which Palladio drew the monuments nor reproduce their appearance or the elements on which Palladio based his reconstructions. For these reasons, a study of the baths drawn by him (and of all the drawings that reconstruct Roman antiquities) must be based exclusively on the original drawings of the monuments themselves, reproduced in the aforementioned volume *I disegni delle Antichità di Andrea Palladio*, published in 1958–59, and hereafter referred to as Zorzi. This is all the more necessary because Burlington has also left out many drawings depicting the same Roman baths merely because they were on large sheets, a fact that should not have prevented their publication.

We know that Palladio did not work as archeologist or copier of ancient ruins, but used his studies of what remained on which to base ideal reconstructions. Thus it is clear that if any particular detail is left out of any drawing reproduced, we cannot judge the reliability of the entire reconstruction of the monument—all of which indicates that we cannot base our research concerning the exactness and coherence of the Palladian reconstructions on the drawings published by Burlington (and still less those of Chameron or Bertotti).

Burlington was unable to identify some of the capitals, column bases, and trabeations published in his work. Moreover, they are reproduced inexactly. First of all, he does not identify a drawing found in his volume, while Bertotti does identify it in figure 16 of his own. The drawing, according to Bertotti, depicts a "part of the plan of the Baths of Vespasian," corresponding to figure 89 in Zorzi, which a partial plan of the baths of Titus, not of Vespasian. The plan of some of the baths in my volume indicated as the "Terme Eleniane," reproduced as figure 144, are not identified by Burlington, or by Bertotti and Chameron. Bertotti judges them "some smaller and less notable baths, whose form Palladio was perhaps unable to distinguish,"[4] but the fact is that these were clearly identified in the *Forma Urbis* in Palladio's time. In addition, Bertotti's statement concerning the other scheme of the baths sketched on the same sheet is completely wrong, since there is an identification in Palladio's hand, reading: "These baths are located at the vineyard of Cardinal Grimani at Monte Cavallo" (today the site is called the Quirinale). Neither Burlington nor Chameron and Bertotti reproduce this sentence.

Another grave omission of Burlington is the lack of a caption on a detail of the Baths of Constantine that is reproduced in another plate of his volume, corresponding to plate 18 in Bertotti. The reason is that, like Bertotti, Burlington has not reproduced the comments in Palladio's handwriting accompanying the drawing: "*Questo è el fiancho de la parte interiore delle Terme di Costantino sopra Monte Cavallo*" [This is the side of an interior portion of the Baths of Constantine on Monte Cavallo], and to the fact that Burlington has not reproduced the writings that indicate areas perfectly symmetric to the central space where the bathers wash. The captions are as follows (see also figure 87 in Zorzi):

a) "*locho dove si lavavano, si nominava il labro*" [washing area, called the basin]

b) "*locho dove si lavavano et si nominava il labro*"

These omissions by Burlington also influenced Chameron and Bertotti. The latter, writing of this drawing which he reproduces in plate XVIII, confessed that he was not able to "find out to which baths it belonged."[5] The most lamentable omission by Burlington is that of writings that label capitals, bases, and trabeations from the Baths of Caracalla (or Anthony) that were instead brought to light by the publication in 1958–59 of all Palladio's drawings of Roman antiquities. Not only are the above-mentioned details perfectly indicated in the 1958–59 volume, but it also appears that those published by Burlington (and thence by Chameron and Bertotti) are drawn quite differently from the originals, which are now kept in the Royal Institute of British Architects in London, having been placed there by Burlington himself.

1) Thus we can see that the Corinthian capital with the corresponding
plan of its base, in volume VI, folio 10, of the Burlington Collection at the 4.1
Royal Institute (also reproduced in Zorzi, figure 121) does not at all correspond to the drawing engraved by Fourdrinier on plate 11 of Burling- 4.2
ton's volume, and therefore not to that on plate 19 of that of Bertotti, as
is seen by comparison of the two designs. The drawing was responsible for
a long and inaccurate comment by Bertotti.[6]

2) Another Corinthian capital with relative trabeation in volume VI,
folio 8, of the Burlington collection at the Royal Institute (also reproduced
as figure 119 in my volume mentioned above) has not been accurately
reproduced on plate 16 and therefore not even on plate 20 in Bertotti, who 4.3
felt the need to add some clarification.[7] Again, Burlington has not even
included the preliminary sketch for this drawing, nor has he included the 4.4
writing that accompanies the original in the collection: "*Questa cornise è de la intrata de là che volta a tramontana et è signata con la lettera B et da le bande de la intrata vi era alcuni bagni*" [This setting is from the entry which faces west, and is indicated with the letter B, and on the sides of the entryway there were several baths]. The letter B is identified in my volume in figure 110 in the drawing of the plan of the Baths of Caracalla, as are the capital and the trabeation to which it refers, at figure 119, on the left side.[8]

3) Another Corinthian capital with superior trabeation in volume VI,
folio 9, of Burlington's collection is reproduced in Zorzi (at figure 120, 4.5
right side), slightly different from that reproduced in Burlington on plate
13 (and therefore also from plate XXIV of the Bertotti volume). Burling- 4.6
ton does not include Palladio's writing above the drawing, which indicates
the source: "*Cornise che va in la nave grande et fa loza ai bagni. Colone*

grosse piedi 2 ½ alte piedi 25 et è segnata con la lettera E" [Setting which goes in the large nave and creates a loggia for the baths. Columns 2 ½ feet thick and 25 feet high indicated with the letter E]. This writing is reproduced in Zorzi. Although Burlington reproduces the original drawing very faithfully, a comparison shows that the details in the original are much more vivid and expressive. Bertotti again adds a comment to the images of this capital and trabeation.[9] However, it is certain that the base reproduced appears also in the original drawing, and since the base is heterogeneous, there is some doubt as to whether the base was found beneath Corinthian columns. In any case, we cannot exclude the possibility that Palladio took it from somewhere nearby, or that the base was under the Corinthian columns at the Baths of Caracalla, given the wealth of pieces and trabeations found there.

4) Besides the Corinthian capitals discussed, Burlington published
images of other heterogeneous orders, all found in the Baths of Caracalla.
4.7 One of these drawings is conserved in London in the collection of the
Royal Institute, in volume VI, folio 10 (left side), corresponding to figure
4.8 121 (left side) in Zorzi. The drawing was reproduced by Burlington on plate 12 (and copied by Bertotti in plate XXI of his volume), but the original drawing is more complete and its indications more precise. The following may be read in Palladio's hand: "*Cornise segnata A che va intorno al cortile che fa le loze da tre bande et da la parte contra la niza li va colone mazore et mazore cornise senza loza*" [Setting indicated with an A which goes around the courtyard which creates a loggia of three levels and at the part with a niche there are greater columns and a larger cornice without loggia]. In addition, at the lower left of the drawing there is a decorated, heterogeneous base, with the following in Palladio's hand: "*Da colona in colona in nel cortile sono distante piedi 7 onze 1. Le colone sono grose piedi 2 onze 1 alte cum basa e capitelo piedi 2 onze 1 ¼*" [The distance from column to column in the courtyard is 7 feet 1 inch. The columns are 2 feet 1 inch thick, with base and capitals 2 feet 1 ¼"]. Although the engraver Fourdrinier meant to copy the original drawing for Burlington, a comparison shows that he significantly altered the original, so that the way in which Palladio worked in drawing ancient monuments and their detail cannot be understood by a perusal of Burlington's volume.

5) Another heterogeneous capital with relative trabeation is contained
4.9 in the Burlington collection, volume VI, folio 9, at left (figure 120 at left
in Zorzi), while in Burlington's volume the drawing is reproduced on two
4.10 plates, 17 and 14, and in Bertotti on plates XXII and XXV. The original

drawing bears, in addition, the following in Palladio's hand: "*Cornise de le loze del cortile descoperto che volta a la parte de tramontana et dite loze é segnate con la lettera G. Le colone é grose piedi 3 onze 2*" [Cornice of the loggia of the open courtyard which faces west; said loggia is indicated with the letter G. Columns are three feet two inches thick]. This original drawing was also preceded by a sketch that is found in the collection at the Royal Institute in volume VI, folio 11, on the right. Within the drawing in Palladio's hand there is a confirmation of the above: "*Questo ordine é del cortile scoperto volto a settrione nel locho segnato G*"[10] [This order belongs to the open courtyard facing north in the place indicated with the letter G]. Said area G of the Baths of Caracalla is indicated on figure 110 in Zorzi. Burlington reproduced the original drawing on two separate plates, because, as he explains, he needed one plate to reproduce the heterogeneous capital, trabeation, and base (plate 17), and another for the cornice, heterogeneous capital, and the base of the column (plate 14). This detail is interesting for scholars, but, as the illustrations show, it is certain that the original drawing was partially altered, by Burlington or his engraver, by the addition of fanciful details, so that it comes as no surprise that Bertotti inserts two annotations, not noticing that they are two reproductions taken
from the same drawing.[11] One last heterogeneous capital with relative base **4.11**
and plan is that represented by Burlington on plate 15 of his volume,
although there is no original for this amongst the drawings in the Royal **4.12**
Institute.[12] Since Bertotti copies the plates in Burlington's volume, it is clear that, by comparing plate 23 in his volume with plate 15 of Burlington's, one sees that he has not only modified the figure of the capital, but also that of the base of the channeled column and its plan.

From all of this information is deduced the absolute necessity of consulting the original drawings, and not the reproduction of Burlington or Bertotti, if one wants to get a clear idea concerning Palladio's work with ancient monuments. In 1949, on the occasion of the fourth centenary of the Palazzo della Raggione of Vicenza, there was an exhibition of Palladio's drawings conserved in London and Vicenza. At that time G. Fiocco recognized that "the study of these drawings presents numerous problems," from whence comes "the necessity of a scientifically accurate publication conducted by a group of scholars coming from the disciplines of art history, architecture, archaeology and paleography. All of these disciplines are needed because the difficulties presented cannot be met by one only."[13]

I thought it opportune to publish all the original drawings by Palladio

or those attributed to him, along with some reconstructions showing how
4.13 the architect, proceeding from his own surveys, was able to rebuild various
ancient monuments in his sketches. It is clear that only the original draw-
4.14 ings allow us to understand Palladio's studies and surveys. It is also evident that the drawings published by Burlington, working with the engraver Fourdrinier, and the later reproductions edited by Chameron and Bertotti Scamozzi, although they bear historical interest, are not authentic reproductions. They do not demonstrate the spirit and the vision with which Palladio drew and reconstructed the monuments. Recently, some scholars have followed Fiocco's guidelines, not only examining the original drawings for their detail, but also working on problems of attribution, using the watermark evidence of the sheets on which the drawings were made.[14] Some conclusions concerning the author of some of the drawings have been made, for example the 1910 photographs of drawings, now regrettably lost, formerly possessed by the Biblioteca Civica of Vicenza, which indicate handwriting different from Palladio's, which I have identified as that of the painter and architect from Verona, Gio. Maria Falconetto.

(1.) C. Chameron, *Description des bains des Romains enrichie des plans de Palladio*, Paris, 1772.

(2.) O. Bertotti Scamozzi, *Le Terme dei Romani disegnate da Andrea Palladio e ripubblicate con l'aggiunta di alcune osservazioni giusta l'esemplare del Lord Conte di Burlington impresso in Londra lanno 1732*, Vicenza, 1810.

(3.) G. C. Zorzi, *I disegni delle Antichità di Andrea Palladio*, Venice, 1959.

(4.) O. Bertotti Scamozzi, *op. cit.*, plate XVII and note on p. 44.

(5.) Id., *ibid.*, plate XVIII and note on p. 44.

(6.) Id., *ibid.*, plate XIX, note on p. 45: "The first [capital] engraved in plate XIX is Corinthian and is decorated in good taste with olive leaves. In order to know what rules were followed in building, there being no scale with which to measure the parts, assume the abacus to be one module and a half in length, with its height being eight parts. The capital can be assumed to be one and an eight modules. If I suppose the height to be one and one-sixth modules, the abacus becomes one and four-sevenths modules long, and its height nine parts of a module, etc." It is clear that this reasoning by Bertotti does not at all correspond to the capital actually drawn by Palladio, which is very different from what he represents. Therefore, his reasoning is completely superfluous.

(7.) Id., *ibid.*, plate XX and note on p. 45: "The second corinthian capital, on plate XX with the trabeation, is a little less than one and a sixth modules high; the trabeation is divided in roughly 12 parts; 4 have the architrave; 3 the frieze; and 5 a cornice, whose overhang is a little less than the height." See the end of the preceding note for comment.

(8.) The corresponding preparatory sketch, reproduced as figure 123 at left in my volume, bears the profile of the trabeation with the writing "This is measured with a Roman palm which is divided in 12 once, each being m. 5." On the other side the decorations on the trabeation are depicted with this writing: "This is measured with the foot of Vicenza and was over the loggia in the entry towards via Appia which leads into the grand courtyard at the front of the middle nave of the Antonian Baths."

(9.) O. Bertotti Scamozzi, *op. cit.*, plate XXIV, note on p. 46: "On plate XXIV there is a Corinthian capital with trabeation, under which there is a heterogeneous base belonging to the column of this capital [?]: it has an overhang one-fifteenth of the module. The capital is one module and seven parts high; the abacus, which is one-seventh of a module wide, is one and one-twentieth modules long. The trabeation is divided into 14 parts: 5 have an architrave, 3 a frieze, and 6 a cornice, the projection of which is a little less that its height. The trabeation is, in my opinion, badly distributed, worse delineated and overloaded with carvings and protuberances."

(10.) This preparatory sketch is reproduced in Zorzi at figure 124, right.

(11.) O. Bertotti Scamozzi, *op. cit.*, plate XXII, note on p. 45, and plate XXV, note on p. 47.

(12.) In the Burlington Collection at the Royal Academy there is another grooved heterogeneous capital with trabeation in volume VI, folio 8 (at right), reproduced in Zorzi, at figure 119, left, which contains the following inscription: "*Cornise dela colona senca loza che va contra la niza grande nel cortile. Le colone sono grose piedi 2 ½ alte piedi 25 canalate con li tondini i li sui piarnici*" [Cornice of the column without loggia which goes against the large niche in the courtyard. The columns are 2 ½ feet wide and 25 high, with grooves, with astragals and plaices]. Perhaps the drawing of this heterogeneous capital of a grooved column was preceded by the sketch found in volume VI, folio 11, recto, right side in the London collection, reproduced in Zorzi at figure 123, where the following inscription may be found: "*Questo capitelo era su le colone intorno al cortile de le terme de Antonio*" [This capital was on the columns around the courtyard of the Baths of Anthony]. This shows that the columns were grooved ones. On one side a heterogeneous base is depicted. However, it is quite hard, perhaps impossible, to demonstrate that this capital was the same represented by Burlington in his plate 15.

(13.) G. Fiocco, "L'esposizione dei disegni di Andrea Palladio a Vicenza," in *Arte Veneta*, III, 1949, p. 184 ss.

(14.) W. Lotz, "Osservazioni intorno ai disegni palladiani," in *Bollettino del Centro Internazionale di Studi di Architettura*, VI, 1962, p. 61; G. G. Zorzi, "Le filigrane dei disegni palladiani delle antichita e alcune attribuzioni a Gio. Mario Falconetto," in *Atti dell'Instituto Veneto di Scienze Lettere ed Arti di Venezia*, CXXII, 1964; G. G. Zorzi, "Gli antichi archi veronesi nei disegni palladiani di Verona e di

Londra attribuiti a Gio. Mario Falconetto," in *Atti dell'Accademia di Agricoltura Scienze e Lettere di Verona*, Verona, 1965; G. G. Zorzi, "Il problema dei disegni palladiani," in *Bollettino del Centro Internazionale di Studi di Architettura*, VI, 1964.

ROSARIO ASSUNTO

THE THEORISTS OF NEOCLASSICISM

For the theorists of neoclassicism who dealt with architecture, sculpture, or painting, esthetic form was a tangible shape given to the thoughts 5.1
and desires arising from any occasion. The shape was characterized by its beauty, sublimity, or grace. It could be beautiful without the qualities of grace or sublimity, or sublime without grace, or with a grace that was merely pleasing to the senses and indifferent to the call of reason. Or again, sublime, but with a sublimity attended by grace and as it were gladdened by it, so one might speak of an uplifted or lofty grace, or indeed of a sublime grace.

The idea of "sublime grace," a widespread but by no means exclusive aspiration of neoclassic esthetics, was set out by Aurelio De Giorgi Bertola, who called on the authority of Cicero and Quintillian in his 1786 *Essay on Grace in the Arts and Letters.* The neoclassicists also pursued an austere sublimity completely devoid of any form of grace, one of many visual modes expressing that culture's temper, aspirations, and certainties as well as a way to satisfy the common wish to renew "fair antiquity." Various images of the ancient world were formed by choosing this or that aspect among many handed down by tradition. The important point to remember is that, whatever its artistic aim, neoclassical esthetics made political loyalties and compromises subservient to itself. Being open to the ancient world, in a Europe aspiring to revitalize the categories of the good and the beautiful, hardly meant disinterest in or escape from political problems. If anything, the opposite was true: forms of political engagement and powerful connections from which most writers, architects, painters, and sculptors derived constant gain, ties that cost André Chenier dearly. (He was guillotined in 1794.) This political involvement was so marked that later sententious critics freely accused the neoclassicists of pandering to authority. The Italian Monti, so harshly judged (*et pour cause*) by the generation that lived through the Risorgimento, and whose actions were the most subject to censure, was probably the most glaring example. Perhaps Giordani spoke the truth when he wrote, in 1830, that when Monti "set himself up as critic of those who try to deceive and subdue the human race, he earned the right to be called a civilized poet."

Giordani himself was the author of "Panegyric to the Emperor Napoleon for his Public Works" whose outline and basic ideas come from his previous remarks, written for the architect Antolini, on the project for the Foro Bonaparte in Milan. These form one of the most important theoretical essays on neoclassical urbanism. The aim was to submit the essay to the emperor himself. Giordani's prose aimed to rehabilitate the unity of the "graceful" and the "sublime" he envisioned with Cicognara and Antolini in their plans and projects. It was to be a vision of Greco-Roman antiquity that was not merely elegiac or based on retrospection. In welcoming Napoleon, French emperor and king ruler of Italy, they greeted the artificer of the longed-for restoration of the ancient sublime grace. He would be aided by the vice-king Eugenio, to which the panegyric is dedicated and whose presence is felt in Foscolo's poem "The Graces." It must be noted that, however paradoxical it may seem, no doubt is cast upon the admiration for Napoleon by the final page of Giordani's brief 1816 essay (where we also find the opinion, dismissed today, that Byzantine art accords perfectly with the neoclassical ideal), which urged the restitution by the Austrian emperor of the horses confiscated by Napoleon from Saint Mark's in Venice. The essay summarizes the historical and artistic subjects set forth in a speech made by Cicognara upon his confirmation, by the Austrian government, in the office of President of the Venetian Academy of Fine Arts, which had already been granted him by Napoleon. We also witness in Cicognara's *History of Sculpture* a change in the second and third chapters, where "the century of Napoleon" becomes simply "the nineteenth century."

With all due respect, one could put forth names far more illustrious than Giordani or Cicognara. Think of the careers of Valadier and Canova,
5.2 or of David, the painter of Robespierre and Napoleon, or of Winckelmann, whose conversion to Catholicism was probably the key that opened the doors of his beloved Rome. The letters concerning his conversation that he wrote from Postdam to his friend Berends on March 27, 1752, and on January 6 of the following year clearly show the spirit with which he dealt with the future Cardinal Archinto, apostolic nuncio at the court of the Polish king. The fulfillment of the *conditio sine qua non*, the conversion to Catholicism, required by Archinto and by Father Rauch, was necessary in order for Winckelmann to remain faithful to what he felt to be his mission, the in-depth study of antiquity. He wished to reveal the sense and the value

of the ancient world, a value that was not merely cognitive but that would show the world "*die reinsten Quellen der Kunst*" (the purest sources of art), for Winckelmann a way to clear the path to a better life and to a higher civilization. For him and his heirs, art exists not for its own sake, but to serve as initiative and synthesis, central to what we call the historical process. To alter one's faith in absolving this mission was dishonesty before neither God nor mankind. Churches and confessions for Winckelmann were of mere instrumental value, means to an end to which he had turned with real religious zeal; merely instrumental, we might say, compared to the religion of ancient beauty and good taste, which promoted morality and happiness for all men.

This profession of faith in the model of ancient art, in beauty as condition for and expression of genuine liberty and the highest morality, of a new civilization, was a further lesson that Winckelmann handed down to succeeding generations. Sovereigns, forms of government, and what we today would call political ideologies were as much means to this end as were Catholicism and Protestantism. The important thing was to restore the absolute values of antiquity; a renovated esthetics that augured a social and moral regeneration precisely *because* it was esthetic, given the central character of that category. In this light (and without the theoretical awareness that we possess today, *a posteriori*) traditional monarchies, the Napoleonic empire, and revolution in all its phases were accepted (or rejected) by men professing the neoclassic ideal—writers, sculptors, architects, or painters—merely insofar as they might help to realize an esthetic project that was also "political," but of a type of politics that went beyond, and above, the limits of various institutions and passed over ideologies with their truths or falsehoods. Institutions would come and go, kings would pass away or be dethroned, ideologies disappear, with others, equally provisional and equally wanting, taking their places—the buildings, public gardens, and city projects would remain, as would the statues, paintings, and poems. It was to be, in other words, a world brought to life and restored to full vigor by the image of the ideal, ancient *polis*: a world where kings, warriors, and statesmen were simply the executors of the projects of artists and men of letters.

One example bears this out. In 1755 (the same year that saw the publication of Winckelmann's "Reflections concerning the imitation of Greek works") Louis XV entrusted the rebuilding of the church of Saint Genevìeve to the architect Jaques-Germain Soufflot. One of the canons of

Saint Genevìeve, Father Bernard, composed a celebratory ode for the occasion in which Soufflot's project was praised and classicist polemic against the rococo was compared to the Rationalist-Catholic dispute against idolatry:

A ses adorateurs la vanité frivole
Semble imprimer le sceau de la fragilité;
Le meme gouffre absorbe et le Pretre et l'Idole.
Ils passent; l'oeil les cherche; ils n'ont jamais été.
La religion seule est stable, est immortelle. . . .

[Frivolous vanity looks like fragility to its admirers, and the same pit swallows both the Priest and Idol. They vanish so thoroughly it's as if they've never existed. Only religion is eternal.] Edited by Fréron, the *Année littéraire* (rebaptized by Voltaire the "ane litteraire") published a review of the ode that defended it as well as Soufflot's building project, which was begun in 1757 and finished by Rondelet in 1780. Most critics began their praises with: "*Personne n'ignore ses voyages en Italie. . . .*" In 1791, the Constitutional Assembly deconsecrated the church of Saint Genevìeve, to dedicate it as national memorial ("*Aux grands hommes la Patrie reconnaissant*") under the name of Panthéon, which has remained to this day. The building has continued to be used as a public edifice in spite of two further, though brief, episodes when it was again used for ecclesiastical purposes: the first under Napoleon I, the second during (and briefly after) the reign of Napoleon III, until 1885. The fortune of this building (whose architect wished to combine the classic ideal with the traditional, vertically oriented French Gothic, mixing pre-Winckelmannian motifs of tranquillity and simplicity with the grandiose, Baroque-classic style of Louis XIV) may be said to symbolize the relationship between art and politics conceived and subjugated to an esthetics for which the antique model was the supreme goal. The ancient world was not merely the goal of art and of the critical or theoretical reflection that, then as now, accompanies and sustains it, but also of a political structure that was at the service of art.

The classic form of that building played an important role in the decision to make a patriotic and republican Pantheon out of the church that Louis the "*Bien-Aimé*" had ordered built, perhaps on the suggestion of the pious Queen Marie Leczinska, on the site of another whose origins went back to Clovis. The classical form, like a presence from antiquity to the eyes of the Constitutional Assembly (many of whom had begun to comb their hair in the manner of Brutus) made the building a worthy contrast to the Gothic medievalism of Saint-Denis, shrine of the monarchy. The taste and desires of Madame de Pompadour, counseled by the likes of Voltaire and Montesquieu, which would become living symbols of the irresponsibility and waste of the *Ancien Régime*, were also behind the classical form of the edifice. In her correspondence concerning it she quoted Homer, ordering her brother, the Marquis of Vendières, later Marquis of Marigny, "Superintendent of Building for the King" and the equivalent, for the Pantheon, of the Abbot Suger of Saint-Denis, to go on a voyage to Italy. His trip slightly predated those of Winckelmann and Barthélemy and resulted in the architectural choices for the church of Saint Genevìeve intended to incarnate the ideal republic of antiquity. Building began just as Cochin, who had accompanied both Vendières and Soufflot in Italy, formulated (as had Winckelmann) what Bauer labels the counter-theory to the esthetics of the *rocaille*, the style of scrolls and shells. These polemical arguments stand out in Winckelmann's "Reflections."

When they chose the name and design, perhaps the Constitutional Assembly had the Roman Pantheon, from which Soufflot took the pronaos of S. Genevìeve, in mind. But most important was the role of antiquity and the modern return to the ancient ideal of sublimity, if not grace. The Roman Pantheon was also evoked more gracefully some decades later in the Canovian temple of Possagno. More than one votive church, from Naples to Milan and Turin, built during the Restoration, recalled the Roman monument, in some cases as a rendering of thanks by sovereigns who had regained their or their ancestor's thrones. For the authors of these churches, if not perhaps for their users, the beauty of the new age, with its hope for peace, distension, and calm grace, after the "sublime" of the warlike Napoleonic era, could be modeled only after the ancient world. Cicognara assented to the Hapsburg Empire not to serve it but to make it serve him towards the realization of his own esthetic ideals and to be able to preside over the Venetian art establishment with the same aim that had led him to glorify Napoleon. Similarly, Giordani, eulogist of Napoleon and orator (1809) for the civil militia in Bologna, offered himself, without success, in a letter to the Baron Cornacchia, Minister of the Interior, for the chair in Greek at the University of Parma in 1817.

Grace as an artistic ideal propelled many a writer, artist, and theorist, professing the neoclassic esthetic, to rally around the Restoration. Some noble exceptions were David, whose reputation as regicide drove him into exile in Belgium, and Foscolo, citizen of Venice, who could not swear obedience to a Viennese emperor who had become the ruler of what had been "his" republic. The neoclassic esthetic that celebrated the Restoration considered grace a quality as distant from any type of sublimity as the Jacobin idea of sublimity (or that of the categorical imperative of Kant) was from all possible forms of grace itself. Neoclassical grace was highly secularized, but not a world of gallantry or feasts, as with the sensual rococo, nor an art of the court. Winckelmann set his concept of grace, that which is pleasing to the reason during everyday life with its demands and pleasures, against this courtly conception. This simpler life was that of the Third Estate, for which, even after 1815, nearly all artists worked along the same esthetic lines in the cafes, marketplaces, private homes, and country houses, or under royal or ecclesiastical commission. "Fair antiquity" was considered the esthetic norm even in workaday existence. And the old gods were evoked in flawless hendecasyllables written to gladden and renew the world:

> *. . .onde per tutta*
> *La celeste materia e la terrestre*
> *Uno spirito, una mente, una divina*
> *Fiamma scorrea, che l'alma era del mondo. . . .*

[. . . when through all heavens and earth a Spirit, mind, or Divine flame soared, the soul of the world. . . .]

> *Tempo già fu, che dilettando i prischi*
> *Dell'apollineo culto archimandriti*
> *Di quanti la natura in cielo e in terra*
> *E nell'aria e nel mar produce effetti*
> *Tanti numi crearo. . . .*

[There was a time when the ancients created gods for all phenomena in the heavens and on earth, in air and sea, and in doing delighted the archimandrites. . . .]

The lines occur in Vicenzo Monti's "Sermon for the Wedding of the Marquis Bartolomeo Costa," in which the domestic Graces, who embellish the everyday world, are invoked:

> . . . *Le Grazie anch'esse*
> *Senza il cui riso nulla cosa è bella* . . . .

[. . . also the Graces, without whom nothing is beautiful. . . .]

In an apostrophe to the bridegroom, to whom the "Sermon" is addressed, Monti mentions the Graces who accompany man throughout life's vicissitudes:

> . . . *gli innocenti balli*
> *Delle Grazie mai sempre a te compagne.*

[. . . the innocent dances of the Graces, who go ever with you.]

In his Sermon of 1825 Monti called on the Graces, embellishment of all life, to oppose the graceless "sublime" of the Romantic imagination, which "*in lugubre color pinge le cose*" (paints things in mournful colors). Yet more than forty years before, in 1781, on the occasion of another marriage, that of the duke Luigi Braschi, nephew of Pope Pius VI, protector of Valadier and future supporter of pro-French sentiment in Rome, member of the civil administration during that city's annexation to the Napoleonic empire, Monti had revived images of the snowcapped peaks of the Alps, smoking volcanoes, and violent storms, favorite visions of pre-Romantic esthetics of the sublime. Kant, in 1770, employed the same visions as examples in his *Critique*, images that might appear terrible if wisdom did not show them to be as beautiful as the rest of nature. A few years before his death, at the height of the Restoration (1826), Monti wrote a song for his wife's birthday that reveals the intimate, family side of neoclassical esthetics. Insofar as it contains the notion of grace, the neoclassical esthetic accommodates domestic sentiments and those that soften the expectation of death:

> *Che nel eterno sonno lacrimando*
> *Gli occhi miei chiuderete.* . . .

[. . . with tears you will close my eyes in eternal sleep. . . .]

The coexistence at this time of Monti's late poems and the neoclassic homes in Posillipo at Naples is worthy of note. The few surviving examples of these houses, as the historian Venditti observes, "document a way of life which today has completely vanished, and which express a coziness and sense of place." The end of Monti's poem also reflects this:

Pregheranno che lieti e ognor sereni
Sieno i tuoi giorni e quelli
Dei dolci amici che ne fan corona. . . .

[They will pray that your life, and those of your friends who adorn it, may be serene and glad. . . .]

Naples was one of the capitals of the neoclassical esthetic from the arrival of Barthèlemy in 1756 to the visits of Winckelmann from 1758 to 1765. Before them, in 1750, Madame de Pompadour had invited de Vandières, Soufflot, Leblanc, and Cochin: the latter would describe the painting in Herculaneum. The minister Tanucci, a friend of Winckelmann's, was sent there in 1755 and founded the Accademia Ercolanense to make the treasures of that ancient city known. Venditti observed that "during the end of the eighteenth century and for some years afterwards architectural production in Naples reached its height . . . with a pleasing ratio between nature and dwelling that more recent buildings have totally lost."

The esthetic governing these more graceful dwellings and urban constructions embodied, in the new environment, Winckelmann's notion of "the calm of the soul" in order that "life may be serene and glad." In 1755, the year of the "*Gedanken*" of the Accademia Ercolanense and of the planning of Santa Genevìeve, Guilliaume Alessandre de Mehegan, admirer of Montesquieu's *L'Esprit des Lois*, dedicated his *Considérations sur les Révolutions des Arts* to the Duke of Orléans. An ideal of the type above was formulated using references to Vitruvian architecture. In the *Considérations* he wrote: "*L'emploi d'un terren ingrat, l'art d'y menager une situation riante, une disposition agréable dans les édifices; une disposition adroite dans les appartements; si ce ne sont pas les talents les plus brillants de l'Architecture, ce sont au moins les plus interessants pour nos besoins et pour nos plaisirs. . . .*" [The use of a barren terrain, the art of providing an agreeable disposition of buildings and skillful arrangement in the apartments: these may not comprise the most brilliant talent in architecture, but are most wont for our needs and pleasure.] Two years later, the English architect Robert Adam, who had already made his grand tour of Italy, explored the ruins of Diocletian's palace in Spalato. Mario Praz writes that from those ruins "and from the stuccoes of the tombs of Via Latina and the loges of our Renaissance," Adam "conceived the idea of an interior decoration which was all grace and delicacy of stucco arabesques, enlivened here and there by colored medallions bearing mythological scenes. . . . the environments no longer served sumptuous ceremonies but were ideal for domestic intimacy, and this neo-classicism in a minor key, having found favor in London, passed, like so much during that season of admiration for English things in the eighteenth century, into France to become the Louis the XVI style." On a page that dates from 1778, Robert Adam himself, joined by his brother James, set out a poetics in which the noun "grace" and its derivatives were paramount: "we have adopted a beautiful variety of light mouldings, gracefully formed, delicately enriched . . . and have added grace and beauty to the whole by a mixture of stucco and painted ornaments. . . ."

It would be useful to take a closer look at how neoclassical esthetics conceived and intended grace, be it "sublime" or "delicate," the latter mild and restful, while grace linked to the sublime tended to be difficult, often heroic. The one quality was seen as an attribute of the other in a fine shading of values, an infinitesimal scale that, analyzed in detail, might form a pleasant chapter in the history of esthetics. Leibniz discussed and described both the delectation caused by unostentatious grace and the proud Jacobin sublime; Kant was stirred by the severe, meditative category of the sublime. But what chiefly interests us here is the formation of grace and sublimity in the many varieties of their harmony and disharmony, as manifestations of the central and determining category of esthetics as it affects the life of peoples and individuals. The awareness of its dominance not only helps to understand the continuity of European history from the middle of the eighteenth century to the years around 1830, a time-span that transformed political events and institutions and that influenced what followed, but also reveals a hidden coherence in the attitudes, shared by many individuals of that time, that at first sight may seem "opportunistic." There is also a strong esthetic sense that seems to pass over politics, only to reveal itself in certain men, who might be suspected of it least, as principally political. Historically verifying the theoretical effectiveness of this central place given to esthetics might indeed be a new way to study the history of neoclassical Europe.

ANTONIO M. DALLA POZZA

RECURRENT ELEMENTS AND MOTIFS IN ANDREA PALLADIO

Recently there has been a surge of literature about Palladio, new and noteworthy contributions concerning specific arguments. Now there is also a more general work that in many ways lays claim to being comprehensive. We refer to Roberto Pane's monumental study published by Einaudi in 1961, which covers Palladio's entire career and is packed with well-researched and accurate information.

The chapter "The Age of the Apprenticeship and First Efforts" contains what are among the most handsome and persuasive pages of the book. Included in the multitude of acute observations in this vast survey, there is, however, a statement that seems at first to be ingenious. Pane wonders about "the value to be given to formal analogies that can be drawn between a drawing or architectural work of Palladio and some previous invention of Serlio, Sanmicheli, Giulio Romano, etc." Having asserted that "such analogies prove a common culture," Pane hastens to add that "we must be on guard against the temptation to use a formal analogy in evaluating the artist, else we run the risk of implying that he lacked imagination."

At the outset this warning seems somewhat finicky. On the other hand, we are frequently reminded throughout Pane's work of numerous similarities between certain structures and themes in Palladio and those of the preceding generation; so much so that we often wonder whether Pane has forgotten his own golden rule. Elsewhere we have described Palladio's encounter with the Bolognese architect and his Treatise a "momentous and determining factor." In Serlio is to be found the essential, though not unique, source of the ideas, technical knowledge, and architectural practices Palladio needed in order to grow from a stonecutter and cornice sculptor to designer and builder.

Serlio's manual taught not only how to plan buildings, but also how to adopt the new, humanistic fashion that had come from Rome to sweep the cities of Northern Italy. His book on Roman antiquity, with its rich collection of floor plans, elevations, and architectonic frameworks, often accompanied by measurements, opened up ancient Roman architecture to the unlearned. It also permitted readers to appreciate the significance of that tradition and to understand the current of renewal that began with Bramante and his school. Finally, Serlio's treatise helped to simplify the rather convoluted set of architectural rules handed down by Vitruvius. Palladio, having discovered his vocation and ready to plan his first structures, must have found Serlio's work an indispensible technical and didactic tool. Although we intend to speak here about this influence, there is no fear of belittling the imagination of the master. Palladio's artistry is based not so much on invention of new forms as on the wide use of existing ones. His emphasis was on relationships and accents. As he himself reported on his experience as architect, "Beauty is a result of the relationship between all the parts, and the parts with the whole; so that buildings should appear single, complete and well-defined bodies to which the limbs converge, each apt to its purpose."

In beginning to discuss recurrent elements and motifs in Andrea Palladio, we realize that the theme might outwardly appear devoid of critical interest, but in our opinion the cultural formation of Palladio is still rich territory. So are the stages of his architectural career, from the beginnings to the great achievement of the loggia of the Basilica. This period, stretching roughly from 1539 to 1546, is not very well documented, in spite of new studies presented on the occasion of the 1949 exposition of Palladio's drawings. We know, through an inscription, that in 1542 Palladio had already built Villa Godi in Lonedo and that one year later he collaborated on the entrance to a building for Cardinal Ridolfi, for which he was paid in 1546. We also know that in March of the same year he presented a plan, with the Maestro Giovanni di Pedemuro, for the loggia of the Basilica. By means of a medal coined to commemorate the event found on the site, we know that Palazzo Civena, later called Trissino, was completed in 1546, having been begun in 1540. It was not until the drawings for this building, kept in London, traveled to Vicenza for the 1949 exhibition that the work was attributed to Palladio.

Doubt concerning the paternity of Villa Marcello in Bertesina (which we have demonstrated, with the publication of related documents, is to be dated no later than 1542–43) was also put to rest on that occasion. Another project in the London collection (reproduced by Pane, page 132, figure 30) and brought to notice by Zorzi as amongst the plans for houses that remained unbuilt, turned out instead, as we have reported elsewhere, to have been built, with some departures from the plans, and is still standing today.

Last is the problem of dating Villa Pisani at Bagnolo. Magrini suggested a date that at first we thought, based on evidence, was incorrect, and we proposed 1559. But afterwards two documents from different sources came to light, dated 1544, which described the building as "palazzo novo." We have, therefore, new information which fills the gap in Palladio's formation and early work and on which further research can be based.

Palazzo Civena

This building adds little to Palladio's fame, being a simple exercise in the style of Bramante. However, it is interesting because of the way it differs from Palladio's drawings. The plans, one beneath an elevation and another two with significant variants, are also of considerable importance.

6.1 The case of Villa Pisani is similar. Existing preparatory drawings by Palladio allow us to follow the planning stages. These can be approximately dated, and the graphical characteristics of structure and line show them to be contemporaneous with other drawings. We are referring in particular to the plan numbered 26 in Pane's book (starting on page 26), and to numbers 29, 32 (with the tripartite Serlian façade), 33 (another project with elevation and façade), 27, the two plans at 38 and 28 (plan with annexed haylofts and loggia), two plans for Palazzo di Iseppo Porto published by Zorzi in his volume on private and public buildings (1964), and finally the elevation, which is doubtless derived from the Palazzetto da Monte. The two elevations, one of four pairs of semicolumns and engaged pillars, Doric and Corinthian respectively, and the other also of two orders (Doric and Corinthian) that Pane labels 42 and 43, must have been finished before the others. We should also note that the entire group during the period 1540–46 (the last year being that of the early plans for the loggia of the Basilica), particularly the writings contained therein, allow a more accurate interpretation of the London and Vicenza collections of drawings of Roman monuments.

The Drawings of Roman Antiquities

Palladio's handwriting is of capital importance in examining the drawings. Zorzi is on the mark when he points out that, for several years, Palladio used the Greek epsilon in place of *e*, as a form of homage to the theories of Trissino, afterwards abandoned upon the death, in 1550, of the illustrious humanist and patron of arts. On the other hand, the indiscriminate use Palladio made of the Greek epsilon, as witnessed by the numerous annotations on drawings of Roman monuments and his plans, points to the fact that Trissino's distinction between a long and a short *e*, for which he adopted two different characters, is lost on Palladio. Anomalies in spelling are not unique to the architect: one of Trissino's copyists, a certain Gasparo Trentino (who on some of Giangiorgio Trissino's account books identifies himself as "clerk of the excellent Master Sir Zuan Zorzo") uniformly adopted the omega instead of our character *o*. Written Italian was anything but stable at this time, and Trentino surely does this to mimic speech, but some doubts remain concerning Palladio's use of *e* because, looking at examples reproduced by Zorzi and dated 1548, that is two years before the death of Trissino, we see that Palladio had given up the epsilon, except in some cases where it is isolated (the Italian conjunction *e*, meaning "and," and the third person singular verb *è*, meaning "he/she/it is"; or else at the beginning of a word).

According to Zorzi, Palladio's spelling varies a great deal until at least 1550 or 1551, after which it appears in some ways to be stable. But it might be more correct to say that it evolves gradually, since the changes can be followed by looking at the manuscript dated 1551 "*addi ultimo otubrio*" (the last day of October) and reviewing previous writings, or by examining writings from the same year regarding Palazzo Chiericati.

A close, patient comparison of the marginal notes in Palladio's hand, especially when considered all together, seems to prove that the explanatory notes and the drawings of the elevations and framework of the Porta dei Leoni and the Porta dei Borsari, as well as the details of the Arch of Septimus Severius, are also by Palladio, although Zorzi, and others before him, attribute these to Giovanni Maria Falconetto. This error leads Zorzi to attribute some sixty drawings in the London collection, previously identified as by Palladio, to Falconetto. We are convinced instead that this theory does not hold up and that, apart from some exceptions such as the drawing of the Maison dorée, all of these drawings are by Palladio, being his own extremely careful, skillful copies of other drawings that he either had memorized or had in hand. Most of these drawings most likely belonged to Serlio, who himself had copied them from originals by Baldassare Peruzzi, Sangallo, and so on, and which Serlio used for his book on Roman antiquities, published in 1540. Such, at least, was our hypothesis in an old article, which we consider still valid. The theory is based on facts which were rigorously checked and are open to investigation.

The proof is that, first, none of the drawings in the London and Vicenza collections that Zorzi attributes to Falconetto or others contains any title or measurement not in Palladio's hand. Second, not only are the plans and elevations of the monuments reproduced exactly as they are found in Serlio's book, even with the same breaks and the same manner of rendering arches in perspective, but in page after page every figure (cornices, frameworks, and so on) bears the same form and number, if not always the same order, as in Serlio. See, for example, the drawing of the Temple of the Vestal in Tivoli, at numbers 194 and 195, which Zorzi attributes to an unknown author of the sixteenth century in his volume *I disegni dell'antichità*. The same architectonic features are found in the courtyards numbered 24, 25, and 26 in Serlio's book:[1] elevation and part of a section, plan, pedestal, beginning of a column, door, one of the windows, and various cornices.

If Serlio omits anything it is for reasons of space. We can see, at number 178 in Zorzi, the same Doric temple called della Pietà, found in Serlio on pages 23–24, or the elevation of the Theater of Marcellus in Serlio on page 46, found in Zorzi at figure 214. It is the same even though in the drawing the spaces between the arches or above the elevation are filled with architectural forms that Serlio omits, instead publishing them in Book IV, which concerns the architectural orders.

The London drawing, in Palladio's hand, with the plan of the Portico of Pompeius (Balbi crypt) is even more convincing. Serlio reproduces the same plan on page 54 of the third book, with references to various places (the Campo di Fiori, Piazza Giudea, and so on) that Palladio reports instead of the letters that Serlio places as reference. Convincing also are the plan and elevation of Settizonio; the Porta di S. Salvatore in Spoleto (autograph drawing note 82 in Zorzi, in Serlio in Book IV, page 51); the Temple of the Sybil in Tivoli (autograph drawing, figure 193 in Zorzi, pages
6.2 32, 33 in Book III of Serlio). The list could include the theaters and amphitheaters (the Colosseum, Arena, Theater of Marcellus, Theater of Pola, Arena of Pola, Theater of Verona); triumphal arches; the plans of some baths (compare Palladio's plans of the Baths of Caracalla, found in Zorzi in figure 110, and the same plan in Serlio in Book III, pages 84–85). The details enlarged by Serlio on pages 86–87 are important. They recur as copies in Palladio's hand, which are reproduced in the volume *Disegni di antichtà* as figures 112 and 113. It is the same with the plan of the Baths

of Diocletian (in Zorzi as figure 126; in Serlio, Book III, pages 92–93). The original drawings by Francesco di Sangallo, dated 1518, on which Serlio's images are based, are conserved in the Uffizi and bear annotations that appear to be in Serlio's hand. Also found in the Uffizi is the original drawing of the Basilica del Foro (reproduced on page 81 in Book III), with the difference that, in Serlio, the image is reversed (the same goes for many other reproductions therein) because it was simpler for the engraver to make a direct copy, which naturally appears inverted when printed. This drawing is attributed to Baldassare Peruzzi. There is also a theatrical scene by Peruzzi, conserved in the prints and drawings collection of the Uffizi, which is reproduced by Serlio (inverted), with slight changes in his treatise above the scenes.

Serlio reproduces mouldings, capitals, and entablatures in abundance: the famous Mecenate cornice, the entablature of the Theater of Marcellus, the cornice of the Basilica Emilia, column bases removed to other sites, the entablature of a piece found near the river Aniene, called the Teverone, near the Numentano bridge. He also reproduces the cornice found "in the foundations of Saint Peter's which Bramante buried at the same site." All of these mouldings, foreshortened and drawn from the same visual angle, recur in the drawings contained in the London and Vicenza collections with the same written annotations by Palladio; often the only difference between them is the inversion of the images.

For his treatise, it seems that Serlio used drawings either in his possession or in circulation by Baldassare and Sallustio Peruzzi, or by the Sangallo faction, that is, by Antonio the Elder and Antonio the Younger, by Giuliano, Francesco, Battista, and Bastiano, or by other admirers of Roman antiquity. It is also clear that Palladio had access to the same drawings, which he patiently and diligently copied, transcribing measurements, captions, and references with such exactness that he retained elements that must have been meaningless to him, as well as spelling traits that he may not have himself possessed. Obviously he could have performed the work over a number of years, as the handwriting would indicate.

This explanation seems to be indirectly confirmed by the fact that drawings of ancient works without titles, legends, or measurements were not in circulation, as seen in the Coner Codex, the Barbarini Codices, or the Uffizi drawings. Now, to continue to believe that those approximately sixty drawings, attributed to Falconetto, do not belong to Palladio, we would have to make the unlikely supposition that they were prepared from scratch by the Veronese architect Falconetto for the sole use of Palladio and that any titles used to label them, with corresponding measurements, followed on other sheets.

The original drawings copied by Palladio probably bore measurements, expressed either in modern or old feet, or in spans, ells, or *canne* (a unit of measure that varied between two and three meters), or even Veronese feet. Palladio did not always translate these last into the unit used in Vicenza. When he did, it must have been not a result of his actually visiting the site, but simply a translation of the various units of measure into Vicentine feet.

The work of copying the drawings held by Serlio and others was probably done around 1540 if not earlier; most were finished before Palladio's first known visits to Rome between 1545 and 1547. The indiscriminate use of the epsilon instead of *e*, as can be seen in several drawings, can be dated from this time. Other examples of handwriting can be found in some supplementary annotations on the drawings of the first and second tier of the Teatro Romano of Verona (Zorzi, figures 222–223), and in Zorzi's reproduction on plate 3, which shows writing from 1548. The complete plans of the Baths, as published by Lord Burlington (which, as we have seen, are not taken from life but are copies of other works) also bear written annotations from the early period and other notes that may be assigned in part to 1546–47, as well as around 1555–54.

The handwritten annotations on a small group of drawings allowing us to tentatively date the works are found in the sketches of Villa Marcellus, Villa Valmarana at Vigardolo, the loggia of the Basilica, another project with a columned loggia inserted into the two extended bodies of buildings, a small set of three or four drawings which, according to a fortunate intuition by Bürger, must be considered "studies" for Villa Pisani, and finally another project, which in a way looks forward both to the Rotonda and to Villa Poiana at Poiana.

Mention has been made of the importance of Palazzo Civena. The actual building differs at several points from the plans, of which we have
6.3 three versions, and the elevation conserved in the London collection. As we and others have noted, the niches between the twin pilasters have been eliminated, and the consoles above the pilasters that hold up the tympanum have been omitted in the windows of the main floor. The windowsills, planned with full parapets, have been substituted by lattice work parapets. The basement floor, with five arcades, was built with soft ashlars with empty rectangular niches in the pilasters and oeil-de-boeufs that are even

with the keystone of the arch. This type of arcade returns more than fifteen years later in the flanking structures of Villa Barbaro at Maser. The contours of the arcades with rustic ashlars present in the drawing (similar to the Bramante-like outside door of the Belvedere) will be used again in the outside portal of Palazzo Thiene and around 1560 for the tops of the haylofts of Villa Thiene at Cicogna, one of which, contrary to the assertions of Pane and other scholars, still exists as it was at the time of Bertotti-Scamozzi.

The angular ashlar-work should be noted in Palladio's drawing. It was not used in the finished structure, but reappeared a short time later as a characteristic motif at Bagnolo, and thence at Palazzo Antonini fifteen years later, and finally in the basement area of Palazzo Valmarana-Braga.

The plan of Palazzo Civena is ordered symmetrically. The drawing contains a rectangular room with apses set in the short sides, with the Serlian entrance placed as a partition between the atrium and the room itself. The project and the building for the Civena family anticipate the façades of Palazzo di Iseppo Porto and Palazzo Marcantonio Thiene, as well as the first two plans for the Palazzo della Ragione. The room in question was never finished, but its shape must have been kept in mind, as well as the element of the Serlian entrance, which is a constant feature in Palladio's work from the beginning. Out of eight drawings made during the first fifteen years of activity, six foresee the use of this kind of room, undoubtedly taken from the plans of Roman baths. Palazzo Chiericati and Palazzo Thiene also have rooms of this type as does the house of the ancient Greeks in Palladio's reconstruction.

The Serlian Doorway

The theme of the Serlian entrance is repeated in six projects. It was not subsequently forgotten, for it shows up in one form or another in the first and second versions of the loggia for the Palazzo della Ragione, in the Villa Poiana, in an unrealized project heavily influenced by Serlio and conserved in Vicenza, in the plan afterwards used for the Palazzetto Da Monte, in the façade of Villa Thiene in Cicogna and the rear of Villa Godi, and, last, for the side of the Loggia del Capitanio. We mentioned that Villa Pisani is to be dated much earlier than was supposed and that the drawings Pane published should be considered preliminary studies, an opinion shared by Bürger. All four drawings have a circular atrium in the form of an exedra, which leads to a staircase inscribed in a circle of respectively convergent and divergent steps, a theme from Bramante made known by Serlio in the third book of his treatise (pages 142–43). Serlio introduces it (in the seventh book, published posthumously) in the façade for the sixth dwelling at the Villa, the plan for which, numbered 27 by Pane, is clearly a tracing.

The various phases of the plan for Villa Pisani have already been discussed elsewhere. The plan numbered 29 in Pane's work must be considered the last before the definitive drawing, in which a loggia, forming an apse inserted between two towers, substitutes one in exedra form. The log-
6.4 gia comes from a preliminary study Pane numbers 28. The dominant motif of the façade facing the Guà is a door, surmounted by a tympanum, with three arches of a clearly Sanmichelian character. A rustic ashlar is placed in relief by the surrounding smooth, white walls of the double towers. This ashlar is made of uniform blocks that form the pilasters. Serlio's influence is behind this kind of ashlar: not only through his book of doors, which appeared in 1551, but also the fourth book dealing with architectural orders. The use of rustic ashlars, where the Roman pilaster blends with a stunted Doric half column, will become one of the main elements of Palladio's early plans for the Palazzo della Ragione, which follows the same
6.5 structure on its ground floor, while the Ionic order on top is characterized by pairs of half columns as in the project for the Civena family and also by the Serlian entry inscribed in a semicircle, as found in various plans for houses and villas.

The fact that the project, reproduced as number 29 in Pane, belongs to the studies for Villa Pisani is proven by various elements and motifs found in the building: the two towers at the sides with identical angular ashlars at basement level, the thermal windows inside the central room and in the main façade, which was originally planned without the external loggia with a temple form. Towards 1550 this form, especially in the Rotonda, grows in importance, while the thermal window reappears in Villa Chiericati in Vancimuglio and later in the Venetian churches. External loggias, however, were probably part of Palladio's thinking before 1550.

The plan of the villa, found in Pane in figure 28, and which Palladio's handwritten notes allow us to date around 1540–45, anticipates not only the loggia in exedra form, with the same type of circular staircase inserted into the main body of the building, but also an external open gallery built around a Serlian entry. Another element found in the preliminary studies represents a unique feature in Palladian architecture: the semicircular staircase. The architect reserves the hexagonal room with niches in unperforated walls, found in the original plan for Villa Pisani, for the four corners of Palazzo Thiene, and for the reconstruction of the casa dei Greci.

One last observation to make is that, in the plan, the two arches that flank the hexagonal loggia may be the same ones Palladio adopts in Villa Godi, on the sides of the stairway and in the loggia above it. The reason for the supposition is that the two projects are in chronological order. There are several analogies between the drawing for the Civena family and the villa built for Tadio Gazoto, afterwards called Villa Grimani, and thenceforth Marcello at Bertesina. One example is the type of window, where the frontispiece is held up by the sill with small pilasters underneath. Palladio uses the same kind of window in the elevation of the plan for a building with fluted Doric columns that Pane publishes on page 120, figure 6. The loggia with three arches at Villa Marcello clearly derives from the Corinthian façade reported by Serlio on page 54 of Book IV. Serlio says that it is a remaking of the second order of the arcades of Pompei. Palladio uses the same motif, perhaps because of the air of nobility it lends the structure, in the upper loggia of the courtyard of Palazzo Thiene, where the artist seems to have had in mind the inner arcades of the Arena of Verona for his rustic arcades, which he will then repeat when building the Loggia di Feltre and others.

Important also is the plan for the villa, found on page 133, figure 33 in Pane. It is also a reinterpretation of the Serlian scheme; Serlio in turn took his inspiration from the "beautiful building" (*bell'edificio)* of Poggioreale. The novelty does not consist of the rectangular loggia with niches inserted in the shorter sides between two foreparts and with access by means of a fifty-five-foot stairway, but in the use of an attic over the Corinthian order.

Villa Valmarana at Vigardolo

The plan of this villa is close to another, which both Pane and Zorzi identify as an unexecuted project, which we instead identify as Villa Bressan di Vigardolo (in Pane, figure 30, page 132). Conceived as a single-storied structure, it was changed during construction to include a second floor. Both the plan and the elevation are significant. In the center, the plan is dominated by a large Serlian entrance with concentric arches, with niched windows, whose Doric columns are dressed with squared ashlars, taken from examples by Giulio Romano though close also to those reported by Serlio

in Book IV on pages 26 and 42 (illustrations of the rustic orders; also in at least eleven types of rustic doors in the volume which Serlio calls "*extraordinario*"). We should also note the peaked roof of the façade, resulting
6.6 in a gable with divided architrave, as in the Temple of Venus in Rome, called also Temple of the Sun and the Moon. Palladio must have had a drawing of this in mind during planning.

In a plan for the villa done at this time, we find instead three Serlian doorways in the façade, of the same type as in the previous drawing: one in the center and two on the sides. A tympanum with a broken arch is above each one, larger in the center (Pane, page 132, figure 32). The source for this type of façade, as for the Serlian doorway with concentric arch, is the Baths, specifically those of Titus, Nero, and Diocletian, drawings of which Palladio must have seen before his visits to Rome.

We will make further observations concerning the plan for Villa Valmarana at Vigardolo later on. For now let us look closely at the plan, rigorously symmetrical and so similar to that for Villa Cricoli that we can call it a copy, although the form is changed from rectangular to nearly square. There is the same distribution of rooms on the two sides and also in the center section. The small pilasters at the four corners of the large loggia, which in the plan has a crossvaulted roof, are characteristic. The same motif occurs also in the lateral rooms in the plan, mentioned above, with three Serlian doorways, also for Villa Valmarana. It was almost certainly taken from the plans of the Roman baths contained in Serlio.

Palladio reused the plan for Villa Valmarana for other projects rather often, especially as regards the placement of two lateral rooms. It served as a template to use with new buildings, as for example in Palazzo Antonini, Villa Sarego at Miega, and, with slight variations, in the plan for Villa Emo.

As for the façade, other commentators have already noted that from this drawing Palladio worked out the façade of Villa Poiana, where pilasters with sharp corners are used for the Serlian doorway. We have traced two documents regarding Villa Poiana that give us dates: we know that in May 1555 the villa was "*nondum finita*" and that in August 1563 the rooms were already "decorated with paintings and gold leaf."

Let us return for a moment to Villa Valmarana at Vigardolo. The niched windows with dressed columns foreseen in the plan do not appear in the finished structure. However, Palladio keeps the motif, taken from Giulio Romano and made popular by Serlio, in reserve for the windows of the external façade of the Palazzo Thiene. The large Serlian doorway is not

built according to the plan either, but in the manner of those made known
by Serlio in Book IV of his treatise and adopted for the loggia of Palazzo 6.7
della Ragione.

For this reason, we must ask whether the execution of Villa Valmarana comes before or after the definitive plan for Palazzo della Ragione. We do not have the documents to answer the question either way. We do know that the villa already existed in 1560, belonging to the cousins Antonio and Giuseppe Valmarana. One very significant architectural motif, however, admits the hypothesis that the construction of the villa took place not after, but before, the beginning of the new loggia of the Basilica. This is a type of vault in the lateral rooms that does not appear in other works of Palladio and that he does not describe in the *Quattro Libri*. It appears to be an early line of research which the architect then abandoned. The dripstones under the cornice of the two architraves of the rectangular apertures of the large Serlian doorway also support the hypothesis. They are nothing but superfluous ornamentation, with a vaguely archeological flavor, discarded in the Basilica, which is built in an extremely spare style.

The double portico of Palazzo della Ragione, begun in 1549; Palazzo Chiericati started in 1551; Palazzo di Iseppo Porto, finished according to the inscription in 1552; and Palazzo Thiene, whose two internal façades were finished in 1556 and 1558 though begun many years before, all seemed, up until a decade ago, the sudden revelation of an artist who had previously built only Villa Godi, dated 1542, in a traditional, provincial style. The gap between these buildings seemed enormous and inexplicable. Now we can safely say that we know most, if not all, of the works behind these great creations, an entire series of buildings to which we can give dates. They are the necessary precursors to the famous structures and represent part of Palladio's growth.

Palazzo Civena, from 1540, although its style is derived from the school of Giulio Romano, is in many ways a significant architectural composition. The different versions of its plan compromise a living texture of archeological motifs and references, such as the atrium with four columns or the apsed room with an arched vault. The façade indicates a first real appreciation of the ashlar, which comes to the fore in Villa Pisani, probably planned in 1541–42, and which prepares the ground for a much greater use of the ashlar in Palazzo Thiene. The latter building unites many elements found separately in previous structures: from Palazzo Civena we have the ashlar, the portal, and the double pilasters at the sides of the external façade; from Villa Pisani at Bagnolo, the loggia on the ground floor; from Villa Grimani-Marcello, the upper loggia; and from Villa Valmarana, the shapes of the second-floor windows in the façade. The same might be said of the early drawings for the Basilica: the use of the pilasters with rusticated ashlars in the arcades of Villa Pisani at Bagnolo in the lower portico and the use of a Serlian doorway from the plan for Villa Valmarana in the upper.

Palladio was capable, in 1540, of creating complex elevations and plans for Palazzo Civena, in line with the new artistic culture, and in 1541 or 1542 he was able to plan Villa di Bagnolo for the Pisani family, where he searches for pictorial effects by means of juxtaposing light, smooth surfaces with rugged ones, contrasting natural and artificial elements. This was the style analogous to that current among the cultivated composers of Latin or Italian verse, who used a highly polished style, or a willfully deformed macaronic form of Latin, or even the dialects of the farmers. If we assign Villa Valmarana to this period, it seems probable that Villa Godi, as we have said elsewhere, should be dated before 1540.

Palazzo Civena and the other buildings mentioned here, placed together as a group from the same period, lead us to believe that a considerable part of the work of cultural preparation and professional evolution, including the study of antiquity and the copying of drawing related to it, had already been done. Palladio afterwards drew on the structures, schemes, and architectural and planimetric motifs acquired during this period to form the language we think of as his own.

(1.) Sebastiano Serlio, *Il Terzo libro di Sebastiano Serlio Bolognese . . . delle antichità di Roma*, Venezia, 1562.

PALLADIO AND NEOCLASSICISM

The name of Andrea Palladio has always been associated with a vision of august serenity, as if the appellation Trissino gave him, from Pallas Athena, the goddess of the olive-tree, had affected his work. The other Palladio, author of the treatise on agriculture, teaches that the olive is a "pure" tree. Trissino anticipated a return to the ancient purity of the Greeks, an ideal that he himself was unable to attain in his verses. In an "*Italia liberata dai Goti*," a nation purged of Goths (the name Trissino gave his poem), an angel would descend and confer the name that called up images of divine peace. And the conversion of this common stonecutter to classical purism by Trissino, himself spurious son of Apollo, reminds us of the words of Hermes as he presents the young Io who, in Euripides's play, sweeps the entry to the Temple of Apollo with a broom of laurel branches: "First amongst the gods, I grant him the name Io." Io responds: "Faithful to the duties I have taken up since I was a boy, I cleanse the threshold of the gods with sacred boughs of laurel and spray it with water, chasing the insolent flock of birds who mar the friezes and the divine offerings."

Andrea di Pietro from Padua, renamed by an angel who is an architectural expert (Trissino has him paraphrasing a rather technical passage from Vitruvius in his *Italia liberata*), was a common man from north Italy. Like Piranesi, also the son of a Venetian stonecutter, Palladio's imagination was jolted by the Roman monuments, which both men associated with the idea of "magnificence." Artists coming from the north were affected very differently from those who had always lived among such treasures.[1] Piranesi began to paint dusky, forceful watercolors. Palladio, instead, began to adopt a sheer white, "the pure chromatic realization of the maximum intensity of light," as Argan observed. Cesare Brandi adds that these elements of the classical tradition were newly interpreted and used by artists enlightened, or thunderstruck, by their rediscovery.

Brandi's complex disquisition is worth quoting at length, because it goes straight to the heart of the relationship between Palladio and neoclassicism:[2]

> The way in which Palladio places the classical, and in general the architectonic, element at the forefront, not in sight of function or out of meticulousness, compels him to make it as original as he can, simultaneously placing it in and out of the context of Classical antiquity. The essence of Palladio's revitalization of classical symbolism, which reaches the limits of abstraction, is his way of condensing its most orthodox figurative structure. When this fermentation or leavening wakes the figures of Roman antiquity from their secular sleep, Palladio freezes them suddenly, transfixing them like pillars of salt. There is none of that plastic continuity exalted by the Baroque, as in the example of Michelangelo. Palladio stops at the threshold after having created the framework. His columns, pillars and capitals have the uniqueness which is normally the province of a statue or of a character in the alphabet.

At such moments Palladio "reaches the sovereign equilibrium, never before attained so perfectly, between image and sign. This is why he brushes against neoclassicism without succumbing to that mortal lassitude of the classical emblem which was perpetuated in the neoclassic Imperial Style."

In order to place architectural elements in favorable isolation, Palladio accents the void of a window rather that reabsorbing it into the plane by the plastic graduation of the moulding.[3] In this manner, the white wall, "sharply squared and frontally situated," is made to advance toward the observer, preventing the façade from becoming "a mute prospectus or spatial interval instead of arbiter of internal-external space, as intuited by Palladio."

> We need only study his two main façades, those of San Giorgio Maggiore and the Redentore, to see how he exalts, almost to the point of exasperation, the prospective framework, forcing part of the pronaos to come unjoined. . . . At San Giorgio the pronaos seems to emerge slowly, like a bel-
> 7.1 lows slowly filling with air. With the Redentore, Palladio dispenses with dividing the main levels into two, and with superb use of intersections instead superimposes four. Projecting the architecture towards the observer rather than ren-

> dering it solid through series of linear perspective is part of the freshness with which Palladio poses the problem of the external as internal in architectonic space.
>
> His preference for pure white is less that of a colorist going for a single hue, than a way to remove continuity from the building; a way of exalting its status as architectonic element, to be placed in the fore and accentuated from its background. Palladio's use of perspective is also a way to remove the building from the context of its surroundings.

The quality of standing out from surroundings would influence the neoclassical interior, no longer considered an integral whole as in the rococo manner, but an environment where each piece of furniture had its own identity. The secret of the enormous success and broad diffusion of Palladian architecture is its exaltation of and powerful expression of caste and constituted power.

The perspective of the church of the Redentore, with its climb of wall behind wall, of pillar behind pillar, and of pediment behind pediment up to
the pyramid of the roof and the steep, swollen cupola resting on the high **7.2**
tambour between the two small bell towers, is like the solemn image of a bishop conferring the benediction on his flock. The variation of the artificially superimposed surfaces imitates the order of papal paraments, with the chasuble over the dalmatic, the latter over the tunic, and the mitre gleaming with gems as climax.

Palladio, in highlighting classical elements, in particular the column, which he draws out of context at the same time as he introduces it into the setting, represents the same phase of the late sixteenth century as do Milton and Poussin. Milton, as I have written elsewhere, "forgets himself to marble," to echo a phrase from the *Pensieroso*.[4] His ecstasy before the ancient world makes his syntax and language take on a marble-like quality, something without equal in the literature of his time, though we find the same quality in the paintings of Poussin. We might add Palladio to this list. The role of the column in Palladian architecture is at once symbolic and tectonic: the column is the support, the fulcrum of force in the moral sphere, vehicle of those ideals of *virtus* and *dignitas* that Palladio expressed in his structures. Etymologically speaking, the Latin *columna* is a derivative of *columen*, *culmen*, that is, culmination, from the same root *cel-* (*cellere*) from which derive *celsus*, elevated, sublime. And indeed the exclamation *O celsitudo*! comes to mind at the sight of the Palladian column.[5]

There has always been an unanimous chorus of praise for the life-enhancing (as Berenson would have said) character of Palladian architecture, starting with Goethe, who observed the architect had "opened all the paths to art and life,"[6] to Nikolaus Pevsner who called Palladio "the happiest and most serene architect of the late sixteenth century," down to the amateur James Reynolds, who spoke of the air of calm, lightness, and grace mixed in the Palladian villa with maximum style and dignity.[7] Criticism follows fashion, however, and today's is to force mannerism on the past, in the belief that there are affinities between our age of anxiety and the era of mannerism. Now, it may be that one can profitably apply the epithet when examining ambiguous or unsatisfactory works, as, for instance, the work of the Elizabethan dramatist John Marston, whose plays have been reinterpreted as the expression of a spirit that oscillates between the tragic and the ironic. Thus his work can be seen as a manifestation of a type of universal frustration that renders them akin to the "happenings" of the sixties.[8] But to see the architecture of Palladio, which indubitably does contain mannerist elements, in this light, as does Bruno Zevi, leads to misinterpretation.[9]

We know that Milizia, although he admired Palladio, criticized the architect because he had substituted an esthetics based on freedom instead of on precept. Despite the fact that the neoclassicists criticized the architect for taking scandalous liberties, for example with the Maser temple, which, as Ackerman has observed, is more rococo than Roman, nothing forces us to accept the conclusion that Palladio was not a pre-neoclassicist.[10] One does not discharge one's right to belong to a trend merely by a slavish conformity to its rules. Certainly if neoclassicism is narrowly defined, as it has been by Brandi, Lionello Venturi, and, I might add, everyone up to the present, as hibernation, in which the classical ideal is frozen in ice, or as "taking on forms without knowing how to read them" (for an example of this conventional view, see Brandi on Canova), then it certainly becomes difficult to establish a relationship between the work of Palladio and neoclassicism.[11] Hugh Honour, who judges the imperial style harshly and, in my opinion, unjustly, has shown how neoclassicism passed through various stages. It seems unfair to apply the marks of the imperial style, seen by Honour and others as empty pedantry, to neoclassicism, a style whose history is more complex.[12] The theoretical underpinnings of neoclassicism were long in the making before it burst into the brief, intense flowering of the imperial style, thereafter coming apart in the ferment caused by romanticism, the seeds of which it bore from the beginning. Its rise and fall is similar to that of the art nouveau a century later, which also flowered after long preparation and quickly faded. The same could be said of the Renaissance, whose roots have been traced to the Middle Ages and whose initial delicate grace became the solemn array of the sixteenth century. W. Friedländer in *From David to Delacroix* skillfully traces the lives of these styles. The return to the ancient world, forming during the eighteenth century, in addition to being dictated by ideals of rationalism (championed by Milizia and Lodoli in Italy), was inspired also by the penchant for the exotic, a yearning for the ideal that was also at the core of the romantic movement. Many critics consider romanticism and neoclassicism to be two sides of the same coin: the return to the primitive is seen as dictated by both rational and sentimental claims. The fact is that romantics and classicists spoke languages that proceeded from the same stock. When the Swedish architect Ehrensvard perpetrated that caricature of the Doric style that is the door to the Karlskrona dry dock, in the name of the "natural" order that had preceded the Doric, the order that expressed primitive architectonic masculinity, was his action so different from the romantics who celebrated the Gothic because the ogive was, for them, the translation in stone of the interwoven branches of trees in the forest, the origin of all architecture? And is not a statue like Canova's *Amore e Psiche*, in which Honour sees the perfect classical expression of the love embrace, to be placed alongside Keats's romantic expression of desire that draws near but never reaches it goal?

Palladio was not the first to discover Vitruvius and Hellenistic architecture, but he was the first to concentrate on its totality of effect. Others before him had taken modules and elements from classical buildings, inserting them as citations in their structures and thus placing them in a different figurative context, like words derived from Latin that appear in the vulgar tongue. Palladio's plan, on the other hand, was to "summarize the essence of the classical in its most orthodox figurative unit, and revive its secular vitality."[13] The artist who had begun his activity using a bare, cubical style without ornament, who through certain types of Venetian architecture, such as the Fondaco dei Turchi, had followed the type of the provincial Roman villa, and who was thunderstruck, after his journey to Rome, by a vision of majestic calm, was, in the fullest sense, the first neoclassicist.[14] He studied to render that totality of effect and in fact rendered, in his works where the classical canon is reincarnated, the solemn and com-

posed vision of antiquity. This vision is not without its soft rhetoric. Adolfo
7.3 Venturi describes better than any other the Basilica of Vicenza, calling Palladio the "poet-architect," and the structure "a triumphant symphony from
span to span of superb arcades, a victorious clangor of tubes erupting from
the open mouths of the arches. . . . It is a vision of the Roman world meta-
morphosed by the Romantic dream, so eloquent that it foreshadows, with
the superior power of genius, Piranesi's pictorial fantasies of the ruins of
7.4 Rome."[15] Palladio's villas in the rich, mild Venetian countryside are like
Olympus come down to earth, and the landscape, glimpsed through white
7.5 columns, seems to be an Arcadia. The candid apparition of a divinity *ex
machina* appears to transform the land by magic, changing Vicenza into a
spectacular perspective of palaces that concludes in a work whose name is
the key to all others: Teatro Olimpico.

"I would like, before I die, to see the sacristy of the Carità and the Redentore, which I have always before me, and to which nothing I have seen can compare in sublimity and majesty." Thus wrote the architect Quarenghi from St. Petersburg in 1812, remembering, on the banks of the Neva which he had decorated with Palladian structures, the works of his idol and master. This nostalgic view of the church reflected in the Venetian lagoon that appears to the exile as a faraway Olympus is the most eloquent tribute to Palladio's genius.

Things change, however, if we view the work through the lens of mannerism, as Zevi does. This is surprising in a critic who follows Croce working out the history of "styles" and of language in the history of architecture. Was he unaware that he places Palladio in a category at the same time he tries to describe his unmistakable personality? For he presents us with a Palladio who is totally different from what we have imagined, a man who is anything but tranquil.

> We are less accustomed to discerning the feelings and sufferings of the maker in architecture as compared to painting or writing. Because Palladio was the century's only major figure to dedicate himself exclusively to architecture, we do not observe in his life the highs and the lows which are evident in the world of Mannerism. But dramatic contrasts exist in his cultural choices: between the Basilica and the Loggia there is a multitude of struggles and reversals, of wide leaps and intellectual qualms, the opposite, in short, of the calm, idyllic evo-

> lution described in the panegyrical writings. In Palladio's buildings the superimposition of the orders no longer obeys the laws of the relation between weight and resistances, nor of balance between the solidity of a volume and the environment which surrounds and defines it.

After having taken up again the idea of a Palladio who "replaces an esthetic based on precept with one based on will," Zevi continues: "Although he normally maintains the elements prescribed by the Romans, Palladio demolishes their relations, not in homage to the Baroque ideals of movement or of spatial interpretation, but because he is putting in stone a gestural vehemence not found in the architectonic tradition. To this end, Palladio appropriates experiences which have their root in the pictorial world."

Zevi uses Brandi's claim that "Palladio's architecture brushes Neoclassicism without reaching its mortal hibernation," and "touches at the same time the limits of perfection and of death." He nearly makes Palladio a precursor of Holderlin in transferring him from the realm of serenity to the purgatory of mannerist existential angst: "In Palladio's superhuman effort towards abstraction and metaphysical sublimation, we cannot help perceiving a deep, hidden anguish; a condition of alienated culture."

Although Zevi does not go so far, Palladio's situation seems likened to that of the painter Van der Goes, whose work has been seen as a reflection of his tormented life, in the manner of a van Gogh,[16] though it would certainly be as absurd to look to Van der Goes for that vortex of color and stroke we find in his modern colleague, as it would to see the whims of a Gaudì reflected in an architect who lived during the sixteenth century. However, once the idea is admitted that alienation and anguish, characteristics of mannerism, provide us with the key to the artist's work, there is a demand for documentation which, failing to demonstrate the alienation of the artist, can however lead to that of the critic himself. I happened to meet recently a Dutch ecclesiastic, in charge of a parish in France, who, having discovered among the paintings in his church one that seemed to him to be an undiscovered early work by Poussin, thought he spied a young chick, upside down, hidden in the folds of a mantle; and from there extended his research to canvasses attributed to the painter. And in all of them he came upon what he thought to be more or less inverted and slightly deformed chicks, which he took to be emblematic signatures of Poussin. Zevi is not so naive, but the case I have cited is an extreme example of the same type of self-delusion. "He illustrates his situation as isolated genius, all the greater for its equivocality, behind an appearance of a calm and often festive adaptation. He treads the path that leads to Mannerism, but which remains barred to others, even the most convinced followers."

In the Palazzo Valmarana, the way of concluding the façade on the sides with the "thundering apparition of two striking statues in *alto-relievo*" is, for Zevi, "perhaps more wrenchingly and agonizingly anti-classical than any other example of Mannerism. . . . It is not surprising that the Neoclassicists criticized the lack of robustness of the outermost spans, since in this lack is the essence of Palladio's evasion. . . . In no monument are the stamps of alienation and sadness so impressed as here: in this terrifying and definitive statement, which is not protest, of the failure of the rational perception of history and of the world."

This is violent language to describe the formerly calm, idyllic Palladio, victim, in spite of himself, of existential anxiety. To Zevi, Palladio behaves towards the Vitruvian tradition like one of Sade's heroes: "The later work of Palladio is characterized by a virulent and profanatory anticlassicism which turns elements of late antiquity to hyperbole, shattering their relations." In the Loggia del Capitanio "an anticlassicist senile rage explodes, using the architectonic limbs, says Pane, as if they were thrown into a new and diverse rhythm, destitute of any compositive underlying framework."

Shades of a torture scene out of *Justine* or *Juliette*: "The Michelangelism is devoid of any function, unraveled. . . . In no other example had Palladio reached the same paradoxical degree of informality." The small circular temple of Villa Maser, Palladio's last work, is "only apparently inspired by the Pantheon," but, instead, "reflects the aggressive, shattered and alienated pictorial style of his old age, a will no longer open to architecture, but to its decay and annihilation." And the same process of annihilation of architecture is supposedly evident in the villas, for example at Maser, where

> the flattened building serves as white comment to the hilly landscape. We witness, in the country works as well, the evolution of a static, classical concept into an "open" vision which extends across the porticoes and secondary structures into nature, taking from it the subtlest topographic suggestions, nearly merging into the texture of the panorama.
>
> The discomposure also affects the urban profile during Pal-

ladio's later years. His anxiety becomes torture and agony, and the buildings, enlarged, the architectural orders worn out, profane the cityscape. His is a monstrous and overwhelming revolt against society, against his profession or, perhaps, the human condition. And yet Palladio is most often rendered homage as a nondescript and simple personality, when on the contrary he is amongst the most dramatic in the history of architecture. What Argan defines as the painterly qualities of Palladian art cannot be understood as synonymous with elegiac release. They are, instead, the result of a post-mannerist and pre-baroque alienation. . . . In the later works can be seen disdain, discomfort and a desire to cause outrage. Having finished his creative and didactic work, Palladio becomes uncommunicative, turning inward. It is a somber period: the estimate he makes of life and the world cause him not only to protest its myths and laws, but to condemn, in the solitary scream which is the Loggia, their inconsistency.

One could not imagine a more existential conclusion, with its evocation of the title of one of the most celebrated expressionist paintings, *The Scream* by Edvard Munch.

What Zevi does, in fact, is to dramatize a passage delineated by Ackerman in much more equanimous terms, where he notes the break in continuity between Palazzo Antonini in Udine, from 1556, which repeats the tripartite type of the villas in the central pediment with relatively spare columns and sides, and Palazzo Valmarana in Vicenza, from 1565–66.[17] Palladio's last sojourn in Rome, in 1554, which was dominated by the personality of Michelangelo, and his contacts with Venice, according to Ackerman,

> change him from the theoretical classicist of the previous decade into a more sensitive draughtsman with ampler views, who goes beyond Vitruvian proportion and decorum, reaching a more sensuous and more complicated style. His last archeological drawing is of the courtyard of the Carità, in 1561. Afterwards he becomes a more pictorial architect, seeking richness of effect in the modulation of light and shade, an ordering of the surface and a variety of color which gives the

buildings done in the last decade the character of the architecture of late imperial Rome.

The Palazzo Valmarana "has been called Mannerist, which helps call attention to the non-classical characteristics of the façade, but also leads us to the error of placing Palladio in an orbit alien to him." Put in these terms, we can make out, in the outer bays of Palazzo Valmarana, not, as Zevi claims, the "mark of the alienated and sad human condition" or a "terrifying and definitive statement, no longer protest, of the failure of the rational perception of history and of the world," but an abrupt change of proportions, perpetrated "with Mannerist irony akin to that of Giulio Romano, who liked to produce architectonic jests in order to make fun of the purists."[18] Rather than suggesting a "solitary scream," the loggia of the Capitanio seems to recall, and was probably suggested by, the slightly suffocating opulence of the arch of Septimus Severus (Ackerman) and by the cell of the Temple of Bacchus at Baalbek.

"Palladio's unusual interpretation," explains Zevi, "may be understood with the aid of sociology. Venetian civilization of the sixteenth century was troubled and uncertain." The critic quotes Fernand Braudel, who compares Venetian society, after the long war against the Turks, the lengthy economic stagnation aggravated by demographic growth, creating unbalances in the countryside, the progressive crisis in commerce, and so on, with the situation in Europe after the end of the Second World War. From such unrest Palladio's inspiration is supposedly "complex and tortured." We will see shortly how the economic situation, correctly analyzed, imposes in fact the ethic of the villa and consequently the unique success of the Palladian type of villa. But before we conclude our exposition of Zevi's thesis, let us see how it has already made its way into popular works like Lionello Puppi's *Palladio*: "It is obvious that the programmatic classicism of the artist is belied by the formal concreteness of works shored by anticlassical elements, proposing solutions consisting of genuine anticlassicism. This stance is so dramatic in the last works that the very use of classical morphology seems to negate that syntactic order. We are in the 'presence' of an affirmation which is purely and solely visionary."[19]

The following observation by Puppi merits more attention, however:

> This process (and in this consists the problem) had to evolve undramatically, or rather unconsciously, in any case always in

> concordance with the wishes of the men who commissioned the works. . . . Even if the Basilica and the Teatro Olimpico are far apart chronologically, in architectural style and language employed, they proceed from the constant dream of restoring to one's "own" society, and in so doing satisfying its aspirations to nobility and decorousness, the "true beauty and lightness of the ancient world." Besides, we have learnt from Gyorgy Luckás that "for our understanding of our present, and for history, the important thing is the image that a work gives us of the world, what it proclaims, while the extent to which all this accords with the opinions of its author is of wholly secondary importance."

In order to understand the fortune of the Palladian style, and its relationship to neoclassicism, knowing whether there lurks an obscure, dramatic alienation behind the calm and elegiac face, as Zevi claims, is of little importance. What matters is that the world takes Palladio at face value and sees in him the perfect incarnation of an idea.

What was this idea? We know that after new commercial routes were opened and Venice lost its monopoly on imports from the Far East, the Venetian upper classes, unwilling to sit and watch their patrimony be whittled away following the conquest of Constantinople by the Turks, turned inward to concentrate on improving the Venetian hinterland and to render it profitable. Old treatises were dusted off with a view towards interesting those segments of society, left inactive due to the fall in trade, in the life of the farm. These were either classical tracts (Varro, Cato, or Columella) or more recent writings by Palladio (a namesake of the architect, author of works on agriculture, and not the same man), Piero de' Crescenzi, and, above all, Alvise Cornaro's *Discorsi intorno alla vita sobria.* They sought to idealize agriculture, to consecrate it ethically and religiously, and to associate it with pacifism, all of which served the capitalistic goal of allowing the upper classes to subjugate the lower in new fashion.[20]

The master who contributed toward creating newly productive lands, founding new villages and churches, was looked upon as a sort of popular demagogue, procuring new souls for the Lord. "I can truthfully say," Cornaro wrote, "that I have given, in this place, altar and temple to God, and souls to worship Him." This is a religious justification for exploiting the masses akin to that of Dutch Calvinism, with its basis on predestination:

riches are the visible token of divine grace and poverty of a lack thereof. Paternalistic ideology—the relationship between master and servant compared to that among father and son—corresponded to the conservative principles of the Council of Trent, and the type of villa conceived by Palladio was the incarnation of the principle of authority, the cosmological center of the estate. This hierarchy was accentuated by the harmonic proportions of the building, by the "eurhythmy" resulting from the "divine power of numbers contrasted by reason," wrote Daniele Barbaro in his comment to Vitruvius (1556). Classical forms and symbolic ornaments "contribute to the greatness and magnificence of the work," wrote Palladio about the Casa di villa degli Antichi; in other words, they reflect, in visible form, the social position of the owner.

The master of the villa was at the center of a system no less perfect than that of the harmony of heavenly bodies that was expressed in the proportions of the building. Palladio drew from Vitruvius and Plato when he declared: "We seek to have all parts corresponding one to the other in every structure, with such proportions that there are none with which we might measure the whole and the other parts . . . as the proportions of sounds are harmony to the ear, thus measurements are harmony to our eyes, which is wont to delight us without our knowing the reason why, apart from those who attempt to discover the reasons for things." By plac-
7.6 ing the façade of a Roman temple on the plan of a Roman house, Palladio created a type of edifice that, because of its eminent and isolated situation, produces an effect similar to that described in *Hamlet* (4. 5. 123): "There's such divinity doth hedge a king." There is a moral meaning in Palladio's pure and solemn architecture.

Two German critics have called Villa Maser an incarnation of these principles, but the supreme incarnation is to be seen in the unfinished Villa Trissino at Meledo, the plans for which are in the *Quattro Libri*, as Ackerman has rightly observed.[21] The villa is placed on the crest of a hill like the Rotonda and combines the function of a belvedere and a farm villa in an imposing crescendo that for centuries was synonymous with magnificence in architecture. Ackerman writes:

> The formal system, highlighted by a new spatial dimension involving both the center and the background, gives his composition its imposing character. Palladio not only uses the rise of the hill to elevate the building, but uses an august sub-

> structure of walls to create a succession of platforms. I think that the idea of using this type of ascent in order to obtain an architectonic effect was suggested by Roman models, in particular the Tempio della Fortuna at Preneste, that Palladio creatively reinterpreted several times. One of these reinterpretations has the same small temple with cupola and porticoes on four sides.

To avoid the association with sacred architecture, Palladio, in a passage of the *Quattro Libri* (II, page 69, chapter 16), justified the colonnade as conferring grandeur and magnificence, as well as showing off the coat of arms of the owner and the cupola, which he took from his own reconstruction of the Baths of Caracalla.[22] The portico is often the only reference to Roman architecture, all the rest being purely geometric according to the notion of the hierarchy of elements.

Villa Maser is a clear reference to the Romans. In the Bacchus room there is a fresco by Veronese that depicts the ruins of a Roman villa, mentioned several times by Bentham and Muller, since, according to them, the landscape decorations inside the dwelling are not, as R. Palucchini and oth- 7.7
ers thought, Venetian country scenes, but evocations of Mediterranean vistas with a view toward associating the countryside around Padova with that near Rome.[23] Small figures of the Pompeian type in contemporary dress recall the itinerants described by Pliny (*Natural History* XXXV), and the past is compared to the present in a way similar to the Villa d'Este in Tivoli, where Rome is reproduced in miniature in a corner of the garden (the "Rometta" of Pirro Ligorio). In this imitation of an imitation that was the Palladian villa (the *tertium comparationis* being Hadrian's Villa), a reconstruction of the ancient social order was outlined by the reconstruction of an ancient villa. This was a utopian ideal, but the utopia was modeled on the past in an attempt to restore the Golden Age. As such it was retroactive and negative compared to the positive, progressive notion of communal life, which did not desire the rebuilding of a paternalistic past through an escape from the cities to the country, but a transformation of the city into an illuminated and progressive community. Thomas More's *Utopia* and Thomas Campanella's *The City of the Sun* offered blueprints of this society. The presentation of the villa and of villa life as a sort of secular paradise (described as a "terrestrial paradise" by Agostino Gallo in his *Dieci giornate della vera agricoltura e piaceri della villa*, 1550), as an Arcadia, or

as an aid to "blessed agriculture," was to serve as instrument of domination, just as religion was thought to be by Machiavelli and others.[24] The utopia of a More or a Campanella looked to the city itself for a solution, while that of the country was a utopia at the service of masters. Anton Francesco Doni in his *Villa* (1566) sees the advantages of the villa solely from the point of view of its owner, involved in the pseudo-activity of the social and sportive stamp characteristic of the upper classes. This utopia reproduces in the country the same relationship between master and servant that exists in the city. The utopias of More and Campanella sought to put an end to that venerable relation.

The calm thrust toward the spectator that we have noted in the typical Palladian construction won it the favor of first the Venetian and then the English elite. It is worth noting that the man who imported Palladianism into England was Inigo Jones, who had begun his career as theatrical costume and stage designer. It was undoubtedly the spectacular aspect that attracted Jones, as it would later draw another famous architect and stage designer, Desprez.

Another quality that helped make Palladianism widespread was its adaptability to climate. The white villa façades were at home in mild as well as inclement climates. Usually different architectures are expressions of the places where they arise, seeming out of place elsewhere; but Palladio, as Argan has observed, has "the intuition of a new space, which does not generate the architectural form, but is generated by it. Thus the form retains its value as idea/object or of mere 'word' which can be instilled into the context of an ever-changing discourse, without losing any of its original philological purity."[25] For if, as Giuseppe Mazzotti has said, "Palladio has worked the miracle of placing an architecture created under other skies in the Venetian countryside, not just dropping it into a different clime, but making it an integral part," the same might be said for Palladian architecture in the rest of Europe.[26] This is possible because the value as signifier is stronger than that of image, sending forth its ethical message no matter where it is placed. The art of Palladio is a translation into harmony of line and mass of one of the two things that filled Kant with wonder: the starry sky above him and the moral law within his heart.

The classical ethical ideal propagated in England by Joseph Addison had found its visual equivalent when the façade of the Parthenon was adapted to domestic architecture. The façades and columns of the great English homes built in the first half of the eighteenth century, the long, symmetrical wings and the harmonious rotundas, in short all the majestic accouterments of the *Vitruvius Britannicus* which at one time had been fit only for the dwellings of gods and for public spaces, had now become the domain of everyday life for patrician families and the upper middle class. Until the Victorian age, every doorway of the endless row of houses on the high-class streets would have its small archway and Doric, Ionic, or Corinthian columns. Similarly, Thomas de Thomon conceived of a plan in the early nineteenth century for the Russian hierarchy in the center of Poltava, where the columns on the façades of the government buildings were numbered in proportion to the rank of their occupants. Thus the military governor had a façade with six columns in the center with a triangular pediment and a high pedestal, flanked by two wings with four windows each on each floor. The supreme commander of the city had six columns on his pedestal but with a balustrade instead of a pediment and wings with one window apiece; the civil governor's house had six columns with a triangular gable separated from an attic by the cornice; and the colonnade was flanked by two small porticoes with two columns each. The home of the vice-governor had six columns but no porticoes, no attic between pediment and cornice; the head of the police force four columns; the postmaster a portico with two columns. Clerks' dwellings and those of the merchants and ordinary citizens were set apart by their simpler architecture.

The neoclassical elysium was only a painted illusion in the Carolinas and in Louisiana in the American South: often, a row of columns was put in front of an ordinary home, like a starched dickie without a shirt, a mask of respectability and decorum, behind which was found a moral world not unlike that described by O'Neill in *Mourning Becomes Electra*. However the Palladian villa is truly represented here since its origins lie more in representation than in commodity. As Goethe remarked about the Rotonda: 7.8
"The space given to the staircases and vestibules is much more than that given to the house itself," and defined such a building "*wohnbahr aber nicht wohnlich.*" Such a villa had renounced interior magnificence, an empty covering as lifeless as a piece of funeral sculpture—a whited sepulchre, in fact.

(1.) Piranesi titled his theoretical treatise *Of the Magnificence and Architecture of the Romans* (*Della Magnificenza ed Architettura de'Romani*), 1761; Palladio spoke of magnificence concerning the "Casa di villa degli Antichi."
(2.) C. Brandi, "Perché il Palladio non fu neoclassico," in *Struttura e Architettura*, Turin, 1971; see especially p. 283 ss.
(3.) M. Praz, *La filosofia dell'arredamento*, Milan, 1964, p. 156.
(4.) M. Praz, "Milton e Poussin," in *Gusto neoclassico*, Naples, 1952, p. 18.
(5.) The importance of this element of Palladian art was very clear to Rudolf Zeitler, who objected to the definition "*pittoricismo vibrante*" applied to the architect (in a letter to me dated November 1961).
(6.) W. Goethe, *Viaggio in Italia*, Venice, 8 October 1786.
(7.) J. Reynolds, in *Andrea Palladio and the Winged Device*, New York, 1948, a book whose promising title belies its content, which is merely a series of enthusiastic impressions of the villas Reynolds was able to visit.
(8.) See the article by P. J. Finkelpearl, "John Marston of the Middle Temple," in *Times Literary Supplement*, 5 February 1971.
(9.) See the item "Palladio" in *Enciclopedia Universale dell'Arte*, 10, 1963. In the quotes from Zevi's texts, the areas worthy of special attention are printed in italics.
(10.) J. S. Ackerman, *Palladio*, 1966, p. 137.
(11.) See *Gusto neoclassico*, pp. 150–54.
(12.) H. Honour, *Style and Civilisation*, 1968.
(13.) C. Brandi, *op. cit.*, pp. 282, 284.
(14.) J. S. Ackerman, *op. cit.*, pp. 106–9.
(15.) A. Venturi, *Storia dell'arte italiana*, Milan, 1940, XI, 3, pp. 342–43.
(16.) By Jacques Levalleye.
(17.) J. S. Ackerman, *op. cit.*, pp. 106–9.
(18.) J. S. Ackerman, *op. cit.*, p. 112.
(19.) L. Puppi, *Palladio*, 1966; B. Zevi, item "Palladio" in *Enciclopedia Universale dell'Arte*, 1963, 10. Puppi (p. 12) calls Zevi's operation "a specific act of historicism."
(20.) This thesis is contained in the volume by R. Bentmann and M. Muller, *Die Villa als Herrenschaftsarchitektur*, Frankfurt, 1970. Ackerman had already illustrated this agricultural revolution (see *op. cit.*, pp. 53–54). The German authors propose to examine the architecture of the villa in a new light, in order to discover, on the one hand, the secularization of earthly paradise and, on the other, an instrument of domination of the masses. It cannot be denied that the book contains some interesting, though rather obvious, theses concerning the state of affairs in which Palladian architecture, in its function as representative of authority, grew and spread throughout the world. But like the Freudians who see sex in everything, so our two authors attribute all to the class struggle. Thus if a text reads "the commerce of men," they understand "a place of business" and not "communication with others"; and if in another place there is mention of a "dominant position," they see an immediate reference to oppression, not a position on a hill-

side. Thus they see the continuation of the Roman and Palladian idea of the villa, symbol of paternalistic authority, in the homes of the industrial magnates of the nineteenth century, which are situated in privileged positions near the factory (to this end they quote a novel by Fontane, *Villa Treibel*). The also see a recurrence of the ideal of *sancta rusticitas* in the Israeli kibbutz, in the ideology of Adenauer, in the garden-cities, and in the penthouses that because of their function as look-outs they compare to the towers in San Gimignano. In the end they are forced to recognize in these phenomena a splintering from an archetypical state that existed ever since man became *homo sapiens*, attempting to improve his surroundings as far as possible in a given environment. As soon as he formed any sort of society, the dwelling of the chief was always distinguished both by position and by aspect from the rest.

(21.) J. S. Ackerman, *op. cit.*, p. 73.

(22.) J. S. Ackerman, *op. cit.*, p. 65.

(23.) Many derive from the prints of Hieronymus Cock (1551) and from those of Battista Pittoni, as Konrad Oberhuber and A. R. Turner have observed (see R. Pallucchini, "I plagi del Veronese," in *Corriere della Sera*, 26 January 1969).

(24.) William will later declare, "God made the country and mankind the city."

(25.) G. C. Argan, "L'importanza del Sanmicheli nella formazione del Palladio," in *Studi e note*, Rome, 1970, p. 90.

(26.) G. Mazzotti, *Ville Venete*, Rome, 1957, p. 105.

ROSARIO ASSUNTO

INTRODUCTION TO THE ESTHETICS OF PALLADIO

The philosopher who wishes to make sense of the esthetics on which the architecture of Andrea Palladio is based must begin with the notion of the preeminence of artistic representation over function that dominates his art and that he expressed in the pages of the *Quattro Libri dell'Architettura*. As has been noted, this preeminence was debased by the theorists and critics representing the rationalist functionalism of the seventeenth century. Lodoli and Memmo expressed their censure, as did Milizia, who denounced, in his *Elementi di architettura lodoliana,* the "pedestals which lie under the columns" and the "columns of different heights above the same plane" as well as the many "frontispieces to the windows and doors" on the declivity of which Palladio often placed "sprawling statues" (the greatest sin from the rationalist and functionalist point of view!).[1] We find it hard today to read these seventeenth-century criticisms without thinking of the early essay of Argan, recently reprinted, where he indicates Goethe as the critic who knew best how to oppose, using his familiarity with Palladian art, the disdain of his contemporaries. This type of knowledge requires a true poet. Today's philosopher would do well to consider architecture as poetry. He might also take a cue from Algarotti who, in the eighteenth century, identified architecture with the plastic arts and with painting, identifying the correspondence between Palladio and the artist Veronese.[2] The notion of architecture as poetry, however, is out of date in the unpoetic age of science into which, according to Hegel, we have been thrown. The idea of architecture as poetry, as it emerges from Argan's rethinking of seventeenth-century positions, certainly helps us to come to terms with what Palladio meant when, in the dedication to the Count Giacomo Angarano, he defined his theory as that of "building well and with lightness." It shouldn't surprise us that a poet and essayist, Hugo von Hoffmannsthal (largely ignored today), wrote the most penetrating modern comment on Palladio in 1903 during a visit to Vicenza. Here are his words, translated by Leone Traverso:

> Vicenza, stormed by palaces, lies at the foot of a hill. Here the

> architect climbed and saw that the summit of this gentle incline crowned the vista, and in turn he crowned the hillock with his most beautiful vision. Palladio built the Rotonda here: not a house, nor a temple, but both together. A giant circular
> room, covered by a cupola, issues through four doors into 8.1
> four vestibules held up by columns. These four vestibules spill outward to four staircases. The entire structure ministers to
> this magnificent Rotonda: the rooms of the house are built 8.2
> into the mainstays, into the arches that lift up that pure, grand circle; hidden rooms covering the front of the Rotonda give on the single, high space; rooms which look out of barred windows are ensconced in the four stairways, like dark slaves who hold that great weight on their shoulders. . . . The stairways create a superhuman outline which confronts the hills, the sea, the plain and the city. . . . The crown of this hill near Vicenza surpasses house and temple. It is rather an immortal signal or miraculously formed cipher towards which the surrounding mounds seem to incline their heads. The impetus of those hills reaches the grand circle, travels around it and its four staircases, and is tamed.[3]

Hoffmannsthal's comment is not merely fantastical musing. Instead, it helps us to understand the idea, one of the focuses of Palladian esthetics and implicit in his philosophy, of nature as model and point of reference for architectural beauty. Another focal point is the study of antiquity, which Palladio came to love, indeed worship, at the school of Trissino and later Barbaro, perhaps through the medium of the Venetian text published nine years before his birth, the *Hypnerotomachia Poliphili* of the Trevisan Francesco Colonna. Some of its contents appear to be echoed in Palladio's treatise: "Today our own vocabulary and mode of expression, along with our own art of building, are dead and buried along with those true men. O hateful and barbarous sacrilege, how you have conquered the noblest part of the sacred Latin treasures, so dignified and yet today so clouded over and offended by cursed ignorance! Which, along with villainous greed, have blotted out that most perfect and sublime work of Rome. . . . O ancient, sacred father-creators, who brought us your divine erudition, under what inhuman invasion we now see you buried!"[4]

Nature and antiquity are in fact behind the theory of the *Quattro*

Libri, where the ancient way of building is the supreme example of "beauty," "grace," and "loveliness," in an "ornate" edifice whose construction is founded on "beautiful proportion." The opposite is Gothic architecture, held to be without grace or beauty both by Palladio and, a hundred years later, by his English admirer Inigo Jones. Goethe, during his Italian sojourn, makes similar observations. Nature, "simple," "true," and "good," which "builds properly," was imitated successfully by the ancients: thus the purpose of imitating nature, and so imitating antiquity, is to achieve a beauty "graceful to the sight, and which looks on graceful sights." The page in the *Quattro Libri* where Palladio describes the setting of the Rotonda is illustrative of his way of understanding the relationship between nature and architecture; that of a poet, not a scientist. His words agree (though of course they differ in style) with Hoffmannsthal's comment above. He furnishes a definition of architecture as dream, as poetry: "the site is one of the most delightful and amenable one could find, being on a small hill with an easy incline, on the side washed by the navigable River Bacchiglione. On the other side there are lush hills which lend an aspect of a great theater, completely cultivated and abundant in most excellent produce and vines. For which reasons the villa, from its loggia built in all four sides, enjoys most excellent views, some near, some far and ending on the horizon."

Thus the protagonists are nature, seen and enjoyed from the villa, and antiquity, represented by the beauty of a classical villa that can be viewed from anywhere in the surrounding countryside. Palladio renders the idea of seeing and being seen with an image of concentric circles: the villa, with its four identical loggia, acts as an ideal point of reference in which the statues on the staircase, the cupola, and the pediment signal the presence of man as principle character in the continuity of art, nature, and history. The building's site in the center of nature, which morphologically matches the circularity of nature or landscape, is an intrinsic part of the villa, as are the neo-Roman porticoes, stairways, and temple frontispiece. The elements from religious architecture, carried over into civic life, lend the structure grandeur and magnificence. The idea of man as the focus of both nature and history is highlighted by the shape of the central plan, reproducing the form of the universe according to a concept of Platonic humanism with which Palladio came into contact during his formative years.

It was Wittkower who rightly emphasized the correlation between the Renaissance preference for a central plan in religious architecture and the philosophy of Cusano, for whom the circle and the sphere are perfect forms:[5]

> *Circulus est figura perfecta unitatis et simplicitatis; Omnis enim diversitas in ipso est identitas; . . . tantum est in ipso principium, quod finis est in ipso principium; Principium omnium quia centrum, finis omnium quia circumferentia; medium omnium quia diameter; . . . erit machina mundi quasi habens undique centrum et nullibi cicumferentiam, quoniam ejus circumferentia et centrum est Deus, qui est undique et nullibi [De docta ignorantia]; In circulo enim, ubi non est principium nec finis, cum nullus punctus in eo sit, qui potius sit principiam quam finis, video imaginem aeternitatis [De ludo globi].*[6]

Cusano's assertions here, and Palladio's concerning churches with a central **8.3**
plan in the *Quattro Libri*, are strikingly similar:

> concerning the form of Temples, in order to serve Decorum, we will choose the most perfect and excellent plan. This is the Rotonda, (being simple, uniform, equal, strong, and proper) and thus we will make round Temples, since this form lends itself to such a use more than any other, having neither beginning nor end, closed within itself, every part being similar to the others, and all contributing to the whole; and, finally, each part standing equidistant from the center. The Rotonda is ideal for demonstrating the Unity, infinite Essence, Uniformity and Justice of GOD. Besides which, strength and permanence is just as desired for Temples as for other types of buildings. For this reason again, the circular form, which has no angles, is said to be the most apt for the Temple.

The theories of Cusano, as found in the *Quattro Libri* in the sections on churches, most probably were known to Palladio either directly or second hand. In any case they could not have remained unknown to his teachers, or to the other humanists with whom he came into contact. Cusano, furthermore, had studied in Padua and was a friend of Paolo Toscanelli, through whom his ideas became known to the Florentine circles frequented by the young Trissino. In addition, the writings of the cardinal were published during Palladio's career, in four editions appearing in Paris, Milan, Strasburg, and Basel between the years 1488 and 1565. But what is striking about the Rotonda is the extension to civil architecture of a form, with Neoplatonic underpinnings, originally intended for religious use. Palladio's thoughts on this matter, as well as the man who commissioned the Rotonda, Paolo Almerico, should be considered more as a consecration of a secular form than a deconsecration of a religious one. The use of a central plan, as well as the pediments of a classical temple, underline the fundamental poetic nature of the Palladian concept of architecture. As for all other art forms, the sacred and the profane in architecture can be mingled only through a poetic vision, transferring the profane to the solemnity and liberty of the functional service proper to sacred architecture and bringing the light of the sacred to those places destined for everyday use. So the architect invests places that would otherwise be mundane with a religiosity and a notion of the infinite within a finite space, according to the lesson of Cusano, for whom the circle is the figure of eternity.

Religiosity, then, is poetic and plastic transcendence of the function through a superabundance of representation and of form over material ("buildings are admired more for their form than their material," Palladio wrote in his report on the cathedral of Brescia). Religious architecture, which is institutionally representative, be it pagan or Christian, was seen by the humanist Palladio as a model for every type of architecture, pagan forms being considered preparation for the Christian. The solemnity of the statues celebrating mankind as historical protagonist, combining art and nature, is one of the elements by which civic architecture is formed in the image of religious construction, reflecting its pictorial, poetic, and plastic modes.

In public buildings there is an excess of representation: I mean in the auto-celebration and self-representation through which the building declares itself a monument and through harmonized variety and numerous ornament. The ornaments of a religious edifice are characterized by clarity and simplicity that represent the One as distinct from the many, and white Light as distinct from other colors, while the public structure requires greater abundance and visibility of sensible ornament that distinguish it from both the church and the private home. It might help to imagine the ideal Palladian city artistically centered around the temple, that is, around religious buildings. In the words of the *Quattro Libri*: "We choose these sites for Temples, which will be the nobler and more eminent part of the city, far from illfamed places; and these Temples stand above beautiful and ornate squares, to which many streets run. Every part of the Temple shall be seen in its dignity, rousing devotion and wonder in anyone who gazes upon it." The transcendence of representation over function, characteristic of religious architecture, whose very end is representation, gives it the central place in the urban plan. Civic structures tend toward auto-referential monumentality, which transcends in its turn structures built for habitation, where ornament may overshadow function but never elevates the building to monumental status. Palladio speaks of public architecture when he says, "They are of greater size, and bear less ornament than private dwellings, and are for use and comfort; Princes can, through them, show greatness of spirit, and Architects may demonstrate their worthiness with beautiful and wondrous inventions."

Beauty, the result of the poetic nature of architecture, passes from the temple (thus called by Palladio in order to emphasize the continuity between Christian architecture and pagan Roman) to inspire public buildings. Argan, in the early essay mentioned above, authoritatively defines this poetic nature as "function within representation and reality within appearance." The passage can be seen as a sort of esthetic hypostasis between sacred and domestic architecture. Thus Palladio gave the ancient, pre-Christian designation of basilica, a religious designation, to the municipal Palazzo della Ragione, which he renovated, boasting that he had built a structure "amongst the greatest and most beautiful . . . that have been built
from antiquity to our day, both for its size, and for its ornament." The **8.4**
basilica serves as a plastic image, modeled in stone, of its very destination as civic edifice and can be seen as a sort of nonreligious panegyric of mankind. This is shown by statues that extend every pillar, transcending their technical function and becoming eloquent, humanistic representation. The loggia, created twenty-five years later, also demonstrates a conception of architectural beauty as the poetic or fantastic in nature (the dream cited by Hoffmannsthal), not "constructivist" or rationalistic. This is the dream that comes to being in a world entirely poeticized, whose ideal parameters can be reconstructed by determining how Palladio, who conceived of beauty as a result of representation transcending function, conceived the passage from sacred to secular architecture—to use a Neoplatonic metaphor, a passage through diverse emanations.

"Form" and "ornament" find their ultimate interpretation in a building that is an example par excellence of worldliness: the theater, in which **8.5**

representation as functional purpose is analogous, in the profane world of civic architecture, to the entirely representative architecture of the church. In the Teatro Olimpico, a place meant for that sort of representation that is one of our secular rites (a counterpart to sacred ceremony celebrated as mass), the ratio of form to material is in itself representative. The wood and stucco are given the appearance of stone and marble so effectively that Bernardo Baldi paid homage to it by speaking as if it were indeed stone. The pictorial element inherent in the monument, culminating in the human figures that complete the columns of the basilica, is echoed in the statues crowning the balustrade that frame the inner portico. These statues are reproduced in the façade of the proscenium, on the two sides of the triumphal arch opening onto other, illusory spaces. Licisco Magagnato defines beauty as representational efficacy, writing that it is "a motif already foreshadowed by Palladio in his theater," and the theory of beauty as representation may be the basis for the use of perspective in the manner of Scamozzi.[7] The French poetess Marie Anne de la Page, Madame du Boccage, a friend of Voltaire and member of various European academies, including the Arcadian, waxed enthusiastic at the sight of "the steps culminating in a grand balustrade on which reign thirty statues of larger than life size, with all the candor of marble."[8] Madame du Boccage's admiration for Palladio dates from the time of her visit to Count Burlington in the villa at Chiswick that he had ordered modeled after the Rotonda. She recalled when the Marchese Capra received her in the "charming castle" that "was the model for those of Marly, Navarra and Burlington."[9]

A mention of at least two of the three phases of English Palladianism (the first after Inigo Jones's return from Italy in 1615, the second after the voyage of Richard Boyle, the third Earl of Burlington) is important in order to understand Palladian esthetics. This is because the Burlingtonian and post-Burlingtonian periods help us understand Palladio's underlying philosophy, tenets those English gentlemen were the first to grasp. They interpreted the villa as a palace in the country and the palace as a villa in the city:
8.6 an ideal unity of antiquity (the city, modeled on Rome) and nature. The country was the place to which the villa brought the luxuries and comforts of the city. The English world, aesthetically ordered with an eye toward Palladian works and with the example of the *Quattro Libri* always present, is a poeticized world along the lines of Palladio's lesson concerning Vitruvius: "one could not call perfect that work which was useful for only a short time, or uncomfortable, and which because of these contained no grace."

Eighteenth-century Englishmen interpreted this idea of grace as durable perfection, utility, and comfort, as is set forth in the *Primo Libro*, where Palladio offers a sort of ideal history of architecture that originates in the "*case de'Particolari,*" or individual inhabitations: "being likely that man, previously, lived by himself, and only afterwards having some experience with help from other men in performing those actions which render him happy (if happiness can indeed be found in this life) he naturally desired and loved the company of other men; wherefore from many houses sprang towns, and from many towns the city and public edifices."

Thus eighteenth-century English society followed Palladio's notion of the "private" and the "public" and conceived political institutions to guarantee the liberty of the individual. The city, the state, and even religion were theoretical and institutional projections of this liberty, reflecting its absolute and inalienable nature. The Palladian villa and palace, therefore, were models for city architecture. The forms guaranteed the privacy of the country villa in the city, this privacy producing good neighbors respectful of others' rights, including that of the pursuit of happiness. The English conceived of the city along Palladian lines and not in the modern manner that is as suppression of the individual by the masses, compared to which the joys and sorrows of a single subject are irrelevant. Thus the city was a way of uniting in order to guarantee individual happinesses. If one aim of cohabitation in the city is seen as a prolonging of that solitude found in the country with its neighborly relationships, the goal of domestic architecture is to make it so that each person builds a comfortable and handsome house for himself, a home that can be put together with others in such a way that there is a coexistence of those singular conceptions of beauty, a coexistence that increases the happiness of all. Luxury and ornament, columns and gables, the intersection of orders or enormous orders, statues, telamons, and the entire formal repertory of Palladian architecture are the components of a form of beauty offered to all, not only to the owners and inhabitants of the houses themselves. English liberal individualism, which is the heir of the aristocratic, humanistic individualism of the clients for whom Palladio worked, aimed to reproduce, on English soil, visions seen during voyages in Italy: the cities, where wealthy and powerful private citizens inspired admiration through architectural undertakings that, because of their beauty, transformed private commodity and luxury into public service.

We see then that the *Secondo Libro* contains not rhetorical formulae but radical declarations of Palladian esthetics:

8.7 The counts Valmarana, most worthy gentlemen, have built, to their own and their country's honor, commodity and ornament, a building replete with stuccoes and paintings. The signor Giulio Capra has prepared the material to build on a beautiful site above the main street of the city, to serve as ornament to his country, more than for his own needs. This house will have a courtyard, loges, rooms and halls, some small, others large. The form will be beautiful and varied, and, as his name deserves, he will gain praise for its magnificence.

Beauty is the most civil and social aspect of the private home, and representation outweighs function. Beauty is the area in which the owner expresses his civic virtue. These concepts are hard to grasp now, raised as we are to identify architectonic virtue with the most coarse utilitarianism, following the dull repetition that "every ornament is a crime" and holding representation to be immoral. The esthetics of Palladio are diametrically opposed to those of a Loos or a Le Corbusier, who conceive of a house as a "machine for living," "made to live in, and not to be looked at from the outside." The latter, less severe assertion is still, from the Palladian point of view, totally antisocial and uncivil, as it makes a house valuable only to those who live therein, with no thought to its external beauty or the pleasure it might give others. Those who live within the city or in suburban areas derive joy from the beauty of housing that is not their own or (just as we inhabitants of modern cities know by our own sad experience) are frustrated by the ugliness or esthetic void of buildings they are forced to pass by every day which nevertheless may indeed be comfortable and solid for the people who live and work within. Even those who must enter these buildings for any reason derive no joy and cannot share the sense of solidity and comfort of the inhabitants. In short, utility, understood as comfort, durability, and solidity (and we know that today much housing is built for the short term, so even durability is no longer sought after) is understood in Palladian terms as the "selfish" side of private architecture, that for which a house remains "private" in its motivation and scope. Only the possessor enjoys the utility, while the beauty, if any, of the house built by a private individual for his own use becomes a public good that all may enjoy. In the Palladian vision this virtue may be enjoyed by those who frequent the apartments of the nobility, the administrative offices, the warehouses of merchants—in short the inhabitants of a city that is "none other than a grand house" whose "inner" beauty also proceeds from the "outer" beauty of its private housing. This is why Palladio announces that to lend beauty to one's dwelling is a kind of civic duty "*massime in Repubblica,*" and one reason why his house for Giulio Capra, together with the chosen site, was supposed to bring "honor and magnificence" to its owner.

By now we realize the importance of ornament, which raises private habitation in esthetic, social, and even moral terms to the level of buildings for public use. The axiomatic supremacy of "representation" (we might say of Vitruvian "*venustas*") belongs not only to the constructive side, to what in the building is representative with respect to what is functional: supremacy of representation is the culmination by which esthetic value forms the basis of the social and civil importance of the building. This cannot proceed from its functional purposes, summed up in the *commoditas* and the *firmitas,* because these have to do with only the users of the building, while beauty involves not only all the citizens of a place but also its guests. And in the Vicenza built by Palladio, Marie Anne de la Page, Madame Du Boccage, and even Johann Wolfgang Goethe (and, in our century, Hugo von Hoffmansthal), not to mention other important figures, were numbered amongst the guests and travelers. We find the same situation with the villas Palladio built outside the city. Here also, representation wins out over function, the only difference there being that the function of contemplation in the country homes is soteriological (in the humanistic and not the ascetic sense) instead of social, even if Palladio gives us to understand that spirits refined by life in the country will be furnished with a more robust sense of civic duty.

Let us look at Palladio's text once more, noting its simplicity:

> The houses of the city lend true comfort and splendor to the **8.8**
> Gentleman who will inhabit them as need be for the administration of the Republic and the government of his own possessions: but he will perhaps derive no less usefulness and consolation from the country villa, where he will pass the remaining time in seeing to and decorating his possessions, and increasing with the art and industry of agriculture; where his body will conserve its health with those activities done usually at a villa on foot, or on horseback, and where finally the soul,

> tired by the agitation of the city, will be restored and consoled by contemplation or the study of literature, like the ancient Sages who often retreated to like places, where they were visited by virtuous friends and relatives, who can partake of the blessed life using its houses, gardens, fountains and like places of repose.

As set forth in the *Quattro Libri*, where Palladio writes of the Villa Barbaro at Maser and the Villa Trissino at Meledo, the plan of the house and the choice of the site, as well as the cultivation done on that site, are intrinsic to its beauty. All this is in keeping with the notion of representation sur-
8.9 passing function. Gardens and orchards are defined by Palladio as "the soul and diversion of the villa" and together with architectural beauty are seen as echoes of natural beauty. They cooperate to make the villa a place where the mind is purged of worry and can forget daily cares, where it finds "consolation and repose" in the "calm attention to the study of literature and contemplation." As with city buildings, beauty makes a private house a treasure for all, and in the villa, the beauty that echoes nature (as an object of contemplation and meditation) renders the farm a place where not only
8.10 the body but the soul is restored and cured—and not only the soul of the proprietor, but of all the inhabitants in the area. The owner and his guests are aided physically and spiritually, and in esthetic contemplation the soul is educated in virtue.

This idea had its roots in the humanistic culture shared by Palladio and most of the men who commissioned his works. That culture held that man is a being whose public and private morality is elevated by contemplation, as both a form of private meditation and discussion with others, a sort of community contemplation. The description of Villa Repeta at Campiglia dei Berici confirms this view: "there are rooms, some dedicated to Continence, others to Justice, still others to Virtue and the Praises; and there are paintings which illustrate these by Master Battista Maganza, a painter of Vicenza and singular poet. All of this has been done so that this Gentleman [the commissioner of the villa], who gladly receives all who come to visit him, can lodge friends and guests in the room of that virtue to which their spirits seem inclined. . . ." Another confirmation comes from the words written for the dedication of the villa that housed the academy founded by Gian Giorgio Trissino, where there is a memory of the conversations that Palladio heard as a youth in the Oricellari gardens in Florence. The dedication bears the subtitles "*Genio et studiis,*" "*Otio et musis,*" and "*Virtuti et quieti.*"

To sum up, we must bear in mind the soteriological mission, in the humanistic sense of the word, of the beauty of the villa according to Palladian esthetics. From the constructive point of view, the villas are both habitation and temple. The Rotonda, built for the canon Almerico in a dominant position in the countryside (just as Palladio desired churches to dominate the cityscape), is the ideal form of a central plan. Thus Hoffmansthal again deserves credit for his critical penetration in writing of the Rotonda, which is neither a house nor a temple, but perhaps a mixture of both: "*Sie ist nich Haus, nicht Tempel, und ist beides zugleich.*" In the humanistic soteriology fundamental to Palladian esthetics, there is continuity between worldly salvation, that which, by the contemplation of rustic life, educates the spirit towards virtue, and religious well-being, which is the province of churches. The beauty of these is similar to, though not the same as, that of city or country dwellings, public buildings, or theaters. The religion of the humanists, shared by Palladio, was not opposed to established religion, but was a radical philosophy of wisdom, virtue, and earthly happiness: for the humanists, that model of wisdom and worldly virtue handed down by the ancient, pre-Christian universe had intrinsic religious value. This was the reason Palladio placed pagan architecture and Christian churches on an unbroken historical line of development.

Recall the ideal city—the realization of what Hoffmansthal called the dream of Palladio—that painting by Canaletto. Here, perhaps spurred on by Algarotti, the artist pictured the Rialto Bridge as Palladio had planned it, across an imaginary Grand Canal, along the banks of which are placed the Basilica of Vicenza and a private Palladian home, with a crowd of statues above the pediments, the balustrades, and cornices. Now join that fan- **8.11**
tastic image with the very real vision that will live as long as Venice herself endures undestroyed by technology: that of San Giorgio, the church of the Zitelle, the Redentore. And imagine, further down on the horizon, not the recent, horrible condominiums of the Lido, but the green hills on which the Rotonda, planned and built near a navigable river, rises. Weren't the boats that Goethe saw from his vantage point at the Rotonda making their way on the waters of the Bacchiglione, from Verona to the Brenta, headed towards the Venetian Lagoon?

This is only a dream, of course, and the Palladian theory, drawn from his writings and architecture, that we have attempted to trace here (in a world hostile to beauty) is also only a dream, even taking into account Hoffmansthal's noble definition of that term. Let us try to think, then, of a theory founded on the supplanting of function by representation, in a century that has exorcised as diabolical the very concept of representation, that holds artifice as its idol, banishing nature with her beauty and grace, and that considers that history which Palladio and his teachers, the humanists, venerated, to be definitively, ingloriously, and ignominiously finished.

However, since our investigation is a philosophical one, we must ask ourselves if the philosopher may be allowed to dream. We know that, in prison, Socrates was visited by dreams exhorting him to become a musician. Perhaps Palladio emulated the musical Socrates, because he was an architect who philosophized as he planned and built, just as the dream told Socrates to philosophize by myth and not sophistries. We know that there are many philosophers (though they might prefer to call themselves cultural operators) today who hold both myth and reason in contempt and pass off as philosophy a reductive, causal science of man. These are the brothers of those architects who have banished imagination and poetry from their profession, who practice a type of architecture using the categories of the exact and mechanistic sciences. The theoretical interpretation, then, of the dream of Palladio might be healthy for the philosopher and might also supply him with instruments that allow him to undertake a new critique of reason. Reason is both myth and *logos* (the *logos* that comprehends myth; myth that is not adverse to the *logos*), and this criticism might include the motives that have resulted in the contemporary reduction of the *logos* in philosophy and architecture to an arid, bitter caricature. It might also help us to counter that view, hostile to nature and to poetry, the stupidity and cruelty of which are more manifest daily, that threatens to destroy man—that dream whose statuary image we see so often at the height of a Palladian building, a building he raised for men—for men, and not for machines.

(1.) See A. Memmo, *Elementi d'architettura lodoliana ossia l'arte del fabbricare con solidità scientifica e con eleganza non capricciosa*, Zara, 1834, vol. I, p. 263; and F. Milizia, *Memorie degli architetti Antichi e Moderni*, Bassano, 1785, To. II, p. 43.

(2.) G. C. Argan, "Palladio e la critica neoclassica" (1930), in *Studi e note*, Rome, 1970; F. Algarotti, "Saggio sopra la pittura" (1766), in *Saggi*, ed. Giovanni da Pozzo, Bari, 1963, p. 92. See also in the same volume: "Saggio sopra l'Architettura," "Saggio sopra l'Accademia di Francia in Roma," etc; J. W. Goethe, *Italienische Reise*, tr. it. *Viaggio in Italia*, ed. E. Zaniboni, Florence, 1948: *Vicenza, Padova, Venezia.*

(3.) H. von Hoffmannsthal, "Sommereise," in *Prosa II*, Frankfurt Main, 1959, pp. 61–62. Tr. by Leone Traverso, in Hoffmannsthal, *Viaggi e saggi*, Florence, 1948, pp. 81–83.

(4.) *Prosatori volgari del Quattrocento,* ed. Claudio Varese, Milan-Napoli, 1955, p. 1116 ss.

(5.) R. Whittkower, *Principi architettonici nell'età dell'Umanesimo*, London, 1962, tr. cit. Torino, 1964, p. 31.

(6.) I am quoting the edition of which Leo Gabriel is editor: N. von Kues, *Philosophischen- Theologische Schriften*, Vienna, 1967: *De docta ignorantia*, I, XXI (vol. I, p. 268); II, XII, p. 396; *De ludo globi*, I (vol. III, p. 234).

(7.) L. Magagnato, *Teatri italiani del Cinquecento*, Venice, 1954, p. 69.

(8.) *Lettres de Madam du Boccage, contenant ses voyages en France, en Angleterre, en Hollande et en Italie, faits pendant les anneés 1750, 1757 et 1758*, Dresden, 1771, p. 121.

(9.) *Ibidem.*

CONTRIBUTORS

ROBERTO PANE, a practicing architect, was a professor of architecture at the University of Naples; a renowned scholar, he was especially noted for his writings about Palladio, Bernini, and the Renaissance in his native Naples.

LUDWIG HEYDENREICH studied art history at the universities of Berlin and Hamburg; upon receiving his Ph.D., he taught in Berlin, Munich, and Florence; he published several books on Italian Renaissance art and architecture, and he was a member of the Scientific Committee of the Centro Internazionale di Studi di Architettura di Andrea Palladio.

MARIO ZOCCONI, an accomplished painter, was Professor of Fine Art at the University of Trieste. His somewhat novel approach to Palladio stressed the decorative elements in the architect's work.

GIAN GIORGIO ZORZI was trained as a lawyer; he developed his avocation—a love of the fine arts—and became a respected and much-published historian of Renaissance art and architecture; he served on the Board of Directors of Palladio's famed Teatro Olimpico and on the Scientific Committee of the Centro Internazionale di Studi di Architettura di Andrea Palladio.

ROSARIO ASSUNTO studied philosophy at the University of Rome; he taught esthetics at the University of Urbino while conducting extensive research into the various fields—and uses—of esthetic theory; he was especially interested in studying how art can be used as a medium of communication.

ANTONIO DALLA POZZA, a trained archivist, was Director of the State Archives of Venice; he also served on the Board of the State Archives of Vicenza.

MARIO PRAZ earned doctrates from the universities of Rome (in law) and Florence (in literature); he held university teaching positions in England (at Liverpool and Manchester) and Italy (at Rome); his translations into Italian of Shakespeare's works and his writings as a literary critic—especially his pioneering work on neoclassical interior design—influenced a generation of scholars.

ILLUSTRATIONS

POLIPHILO QUIVI NARRA CHE GLI PARVE ANCORA DI DORMIRE ET ALTRONDE IN SOMNO RITROVARSE IN UNA CONVALLE, LA QUALE NEL FINE ERA SERATA DE UNA MIRABILE CLAUSURA CUM UNA PORTENTOSA PYRAMIDE DE ADMIRATIONE DIGNA ET UNO EXCELSO OBELISCO DE SOPRA. LA QUALE CUM DILIGENTIA ET PIACERE SUBTILMENTE LA CONSIDEROE.

LA SPAVENTEVOLE SILVA ET CONSTIpato nemore evaso et gli primi altri lochi, per el dolce somno che se havea per le fesse et prosternate membre diffuso, relicti, me ritrovai di novo in uno più delectabile sito assai più che el praecedente. El quale non era de monti horridi et crepidinose rupe intorniato né falcato' di strumosi iugi, ma compositamente de grate montagniole di non tropo altecia, silvose di giovani quercioli, di roburi, fraxini et carpini et di frondosi esculi et ilice et di teneri coryli et di alni et di tilie et di opio' et de infructuosi oleastri, dispositi secondo l'aspecto de gli arboriferi colli. Et giù al pia-

1.1

12

1.2

innodati fili aurei ingemmati pandavano al praefato modo [illegible] et ordine, ma di numero nove, nel medio cum gratioso inflexo curvescenti; la platina, intro et di fora, cum semiexplicatura de excellentissimo expresso di pueruli, monstriculi, fiori et foliamento copiosamente decorata; et il tuto spectatissimo et mirabile artificio se praestava. Dinanti dunque alla praescripta et sacratissima ara de incredibile impensa et artificio, di subito la intenta sacerdotula admonita, dirinpecto alla sacrificante Polia cum il rituale libro aperto, venerabonda se apresentoe. Et tute, seclusa la antistite, per quello modo al lapilloso solo sumptuoso et luculeo cernuamente geniculate et in quest·a· celebre et solenne eusebia,' cum voce divote et tremule supplicante sentivi, cum tale oratione le tre divine Gratie invocare legendo:

1.3

1.1 *Hypnerotomachia Poliphili*, page 12
1.2 *Hypnerotomachia Poliphili*, page 343; detail
1.3 *Hypnerotomachia Poliphili*, page 217
1.4 S. Serlio, The Colosseum
1.5 A. Palladio, Temple of Mars the Avenger (*The Four Books*)

DELLE ANTICHITA.
LIBRO TERZO.
70
PIANTA QVARTA
QVESTO SPACIO DA SAETTA A SAETTA ERANO GRADI DOVE SEDEVANO LI SPETATORI COMODAMENTE
PIANTA TERZA
LVMI
PIANTA PRIMA
GRADI CO SIINCAST RATI
SCALE FRA LI GRADI

1.4

LIBRO
QVARTO

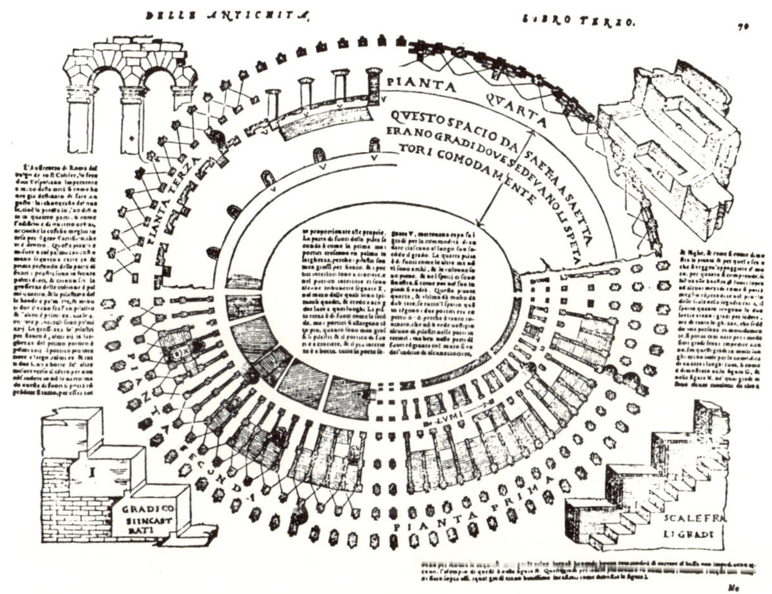

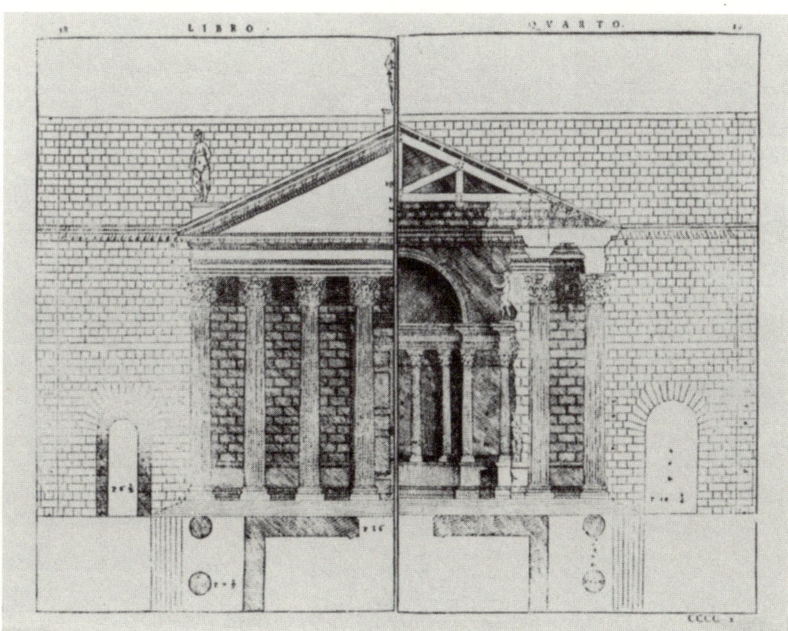

1.5

1.6 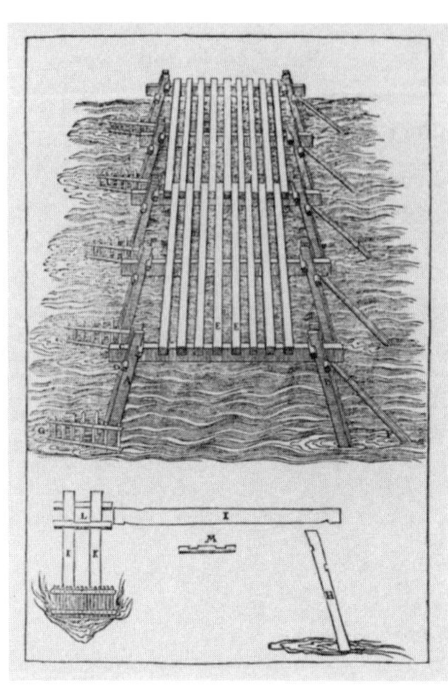

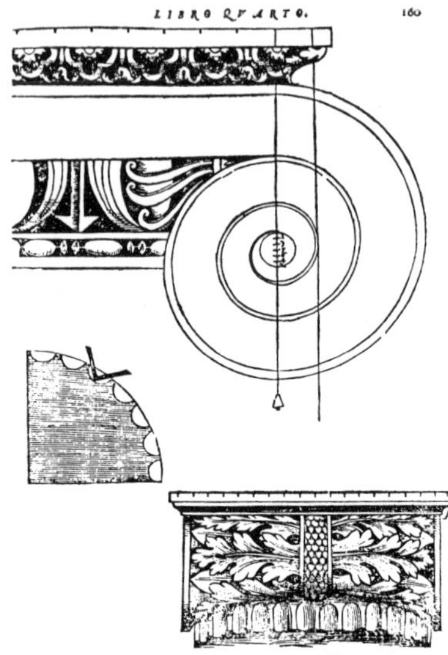 1.7

1.8 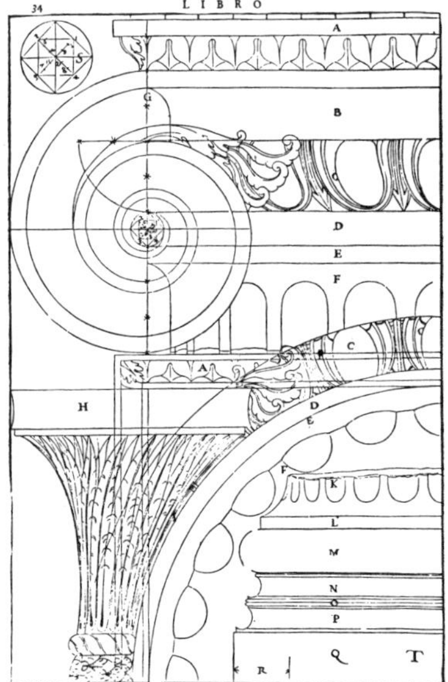

1.6 A. Palladio, Bridge on the Rhine (*The Four Books*)
1.7 S. Serlio, Ionic capitol
1.8 A. Palladio, Ionic capitol (*The Four Books*)

di: e dico due; perche quello, che uà ſotto terra per le cantine, e ſimili uſi, e quello che vä nella parte di ſopra, e ſerue per granari, e mezati non chiamo ordine principale, per non darſi all'habitatione de' Gentil'huomini.

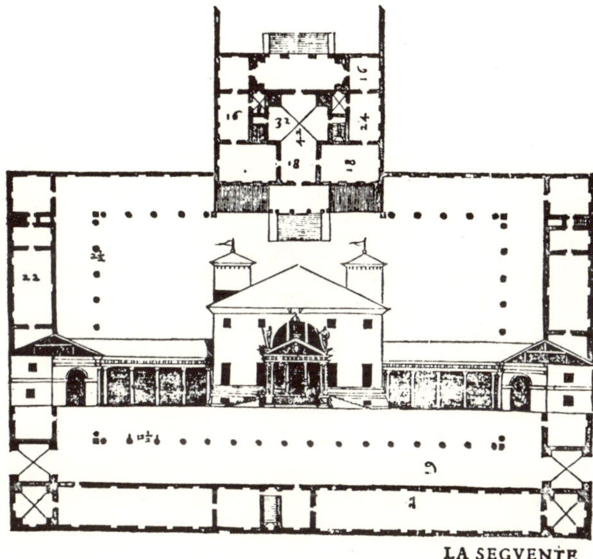

1.9

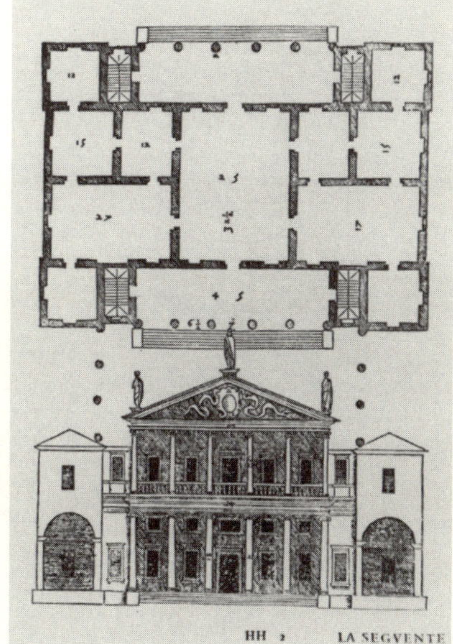

1.10

1.9 A. Palladio, Villa Pisani at Bagnolo (*The Four Books*)
1.10 A. Palladio, Villa Valmarana at Lisiera (*The Four Books*)

1.11

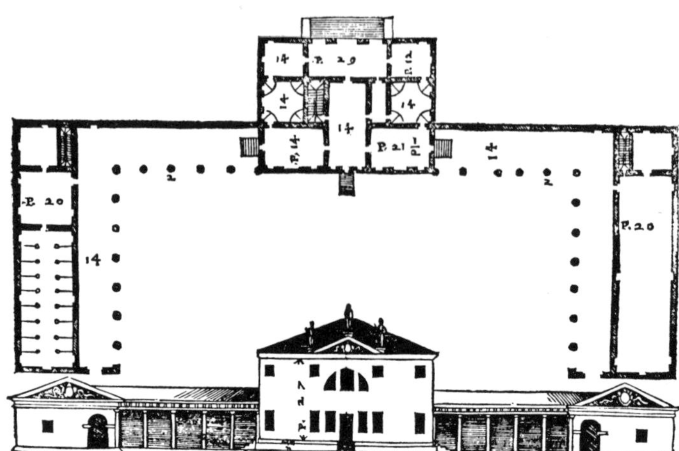

1.12

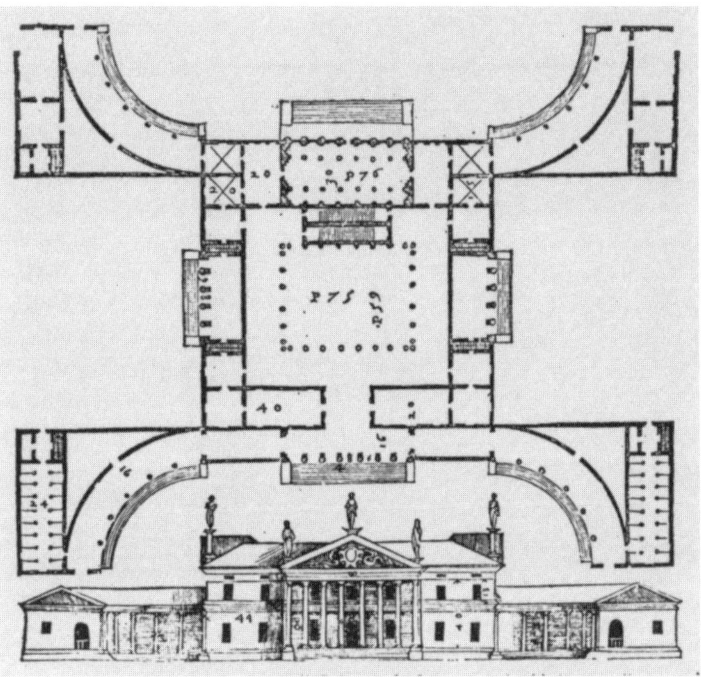

1.11 A. Palladio, Villa Zeno at Cessalto (*The Four Books*)
1.12 A. Palladio, Villa Mocenigo sulla Brenta (*The Four Books*)

2.1

2.2

2.1 Villa Medici Careggi
2.2 Villia Medici at Fiesole

2.3 Poggio Reale
2.4 Villa Medici at Poggio a Caiano
2.5 G. Da Sangallo, Villa Medici at Poggio a Caiano
2.6 The Sforzesca near Vigevano

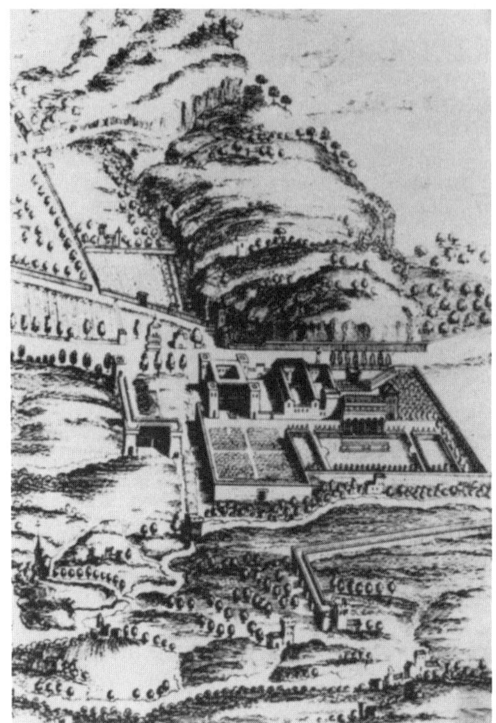

2.3

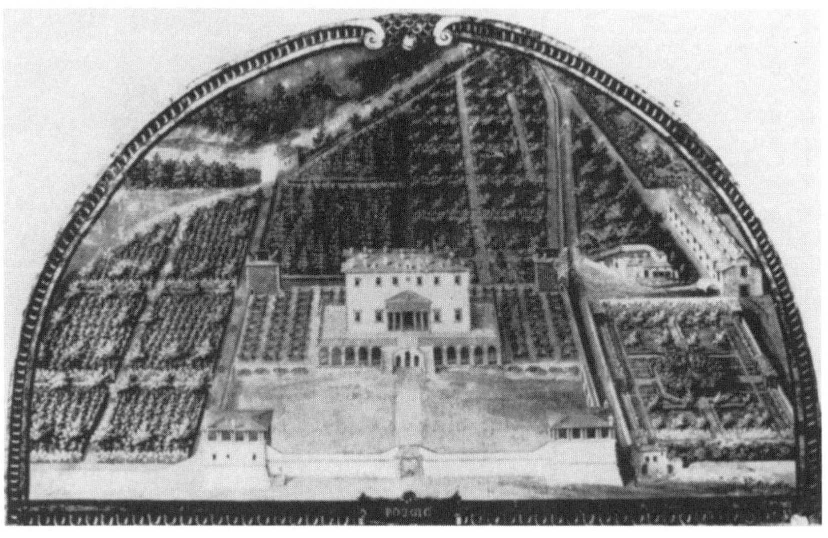

2.4

2.5

2.6

2.7 

2.8 

2.7 The Cascina near Poggio a Caiano

2.8 A. Lorensetti, "Effects of Good Government," Palazzo Pubblico, Siena; detail

2.9 The Cascina near Poggio a Caiano; plan
2.10 Villa dei Misteri, Pompeii

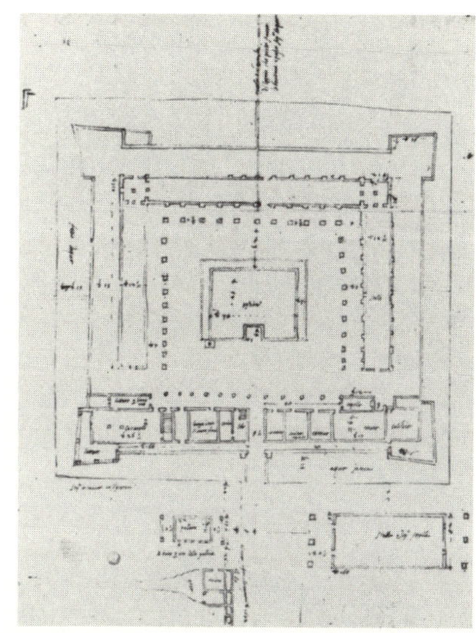

2.9

2.10

2.11

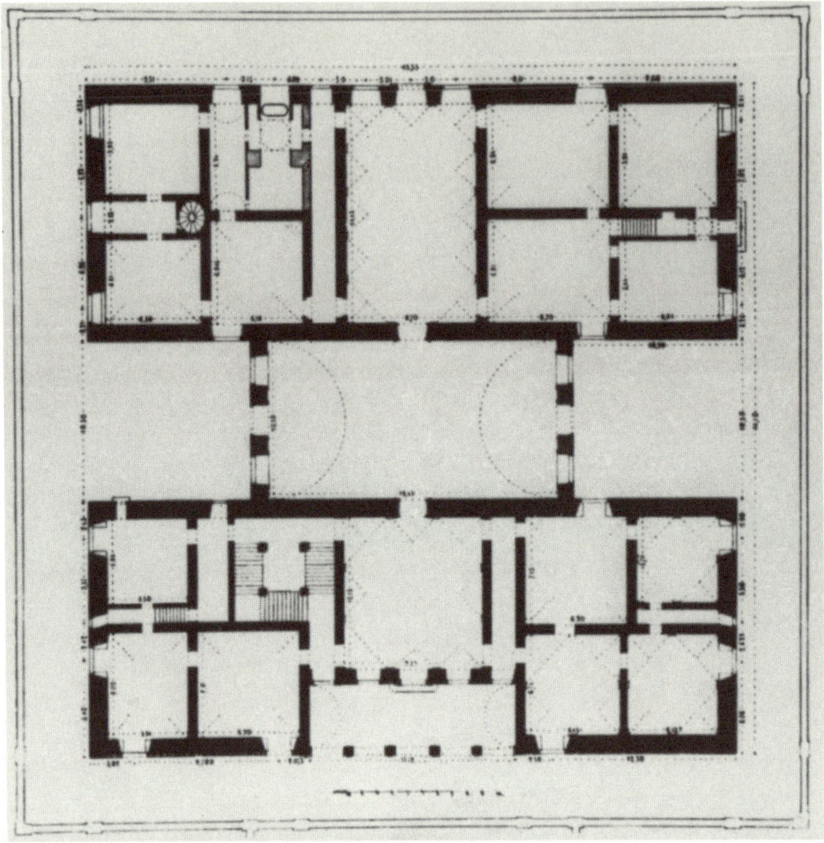

2.12

2.11 Villa Medici at Poggio a Caino; plan
2.12 Villa Medici at Poggio a Caino; detail of frieze

2.13

2.14

2.13 Raphael, Villa Madama, Rome
2.14 Palazzo Colonna, Palestrina

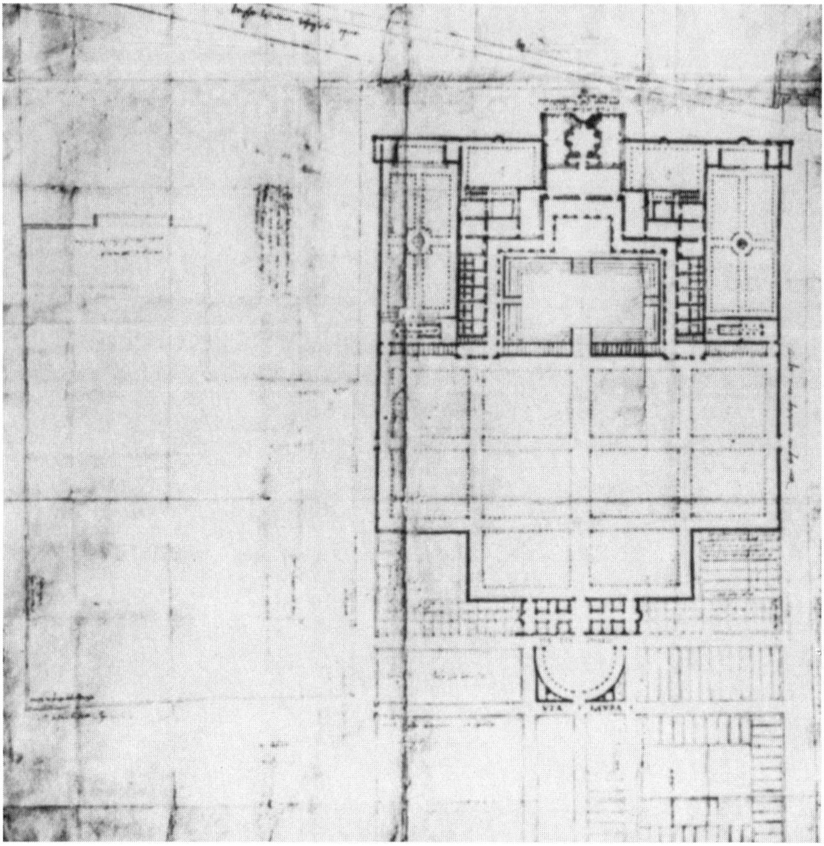

2.15

2.16

2.17

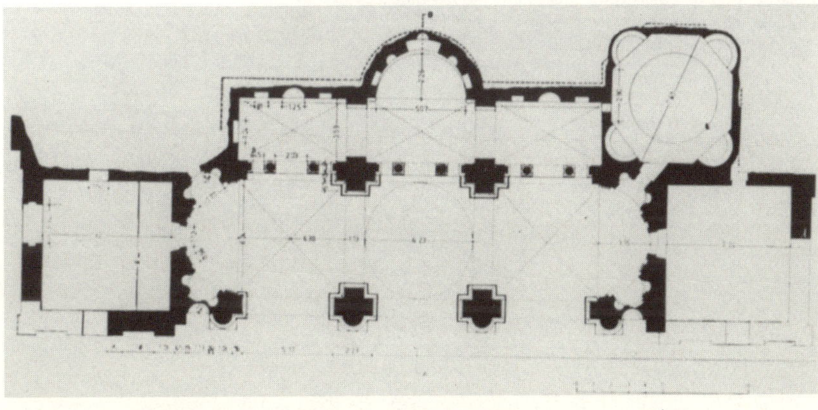

2.18

2.15 A. Da Sangallo, suburban villa at Florence
2.16 Ninfeo at Genazzano; detail
2.17 Ninfeo at Genazzano; interior
2.18 Ninfeo at Genazzano; plan

2.19

2.19 Ca' Brusa
2.20 Villa Colleoni at Thiene
2.21 Villa Trissino at Cricoli

2.20

2.21

2.22

2.22 Villa dei Vescovi
2.23 J. Sansovino, Villa Garzoni

2.23

3.1

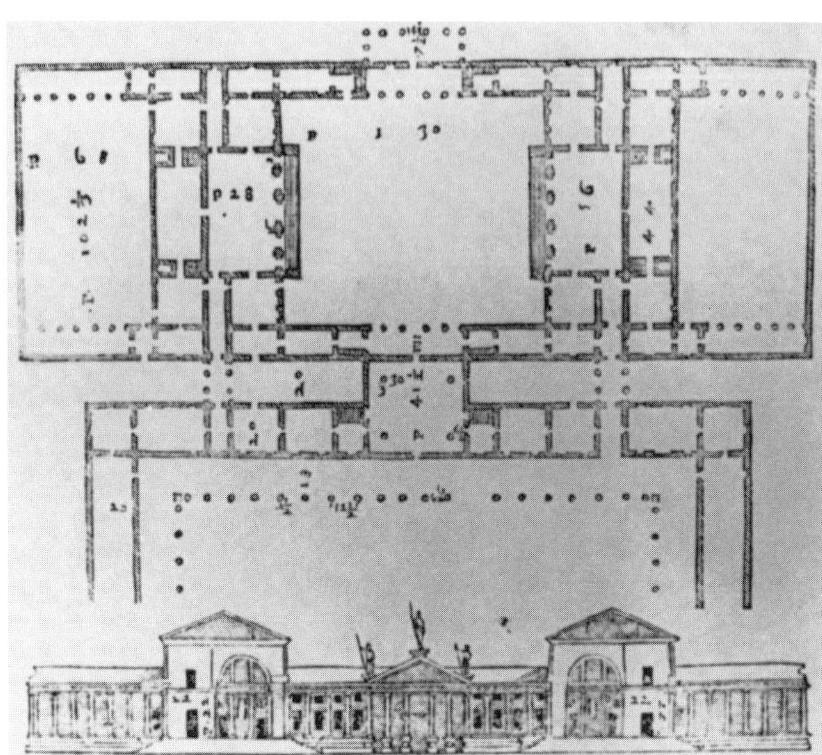

3.2

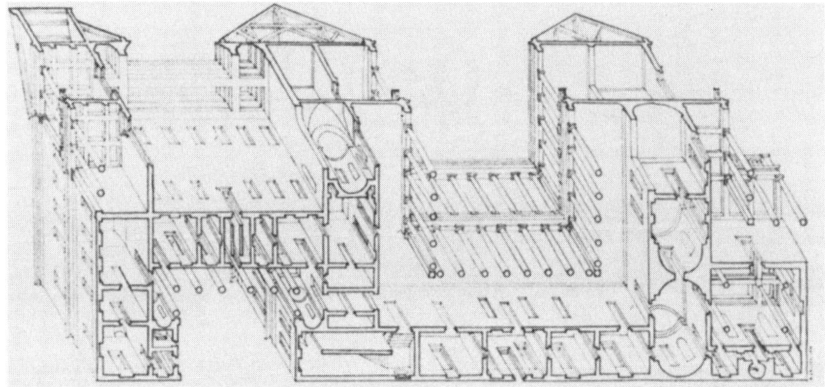

3.1 A. Palladio, Villa Trissino at Quinto; plan and façade (*The Four Books*)
3.2 A. Palladio, *Casa degli Antichi*; isometric (*The Four Books*)

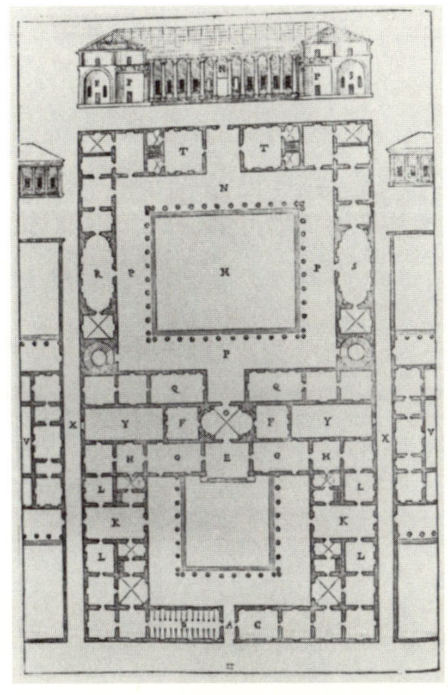

3.3

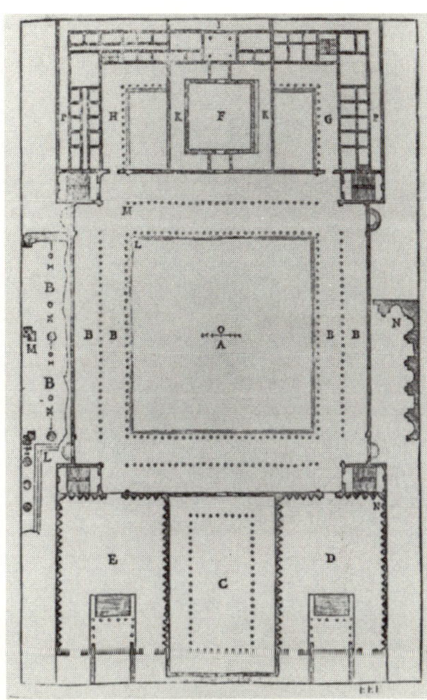

3.4

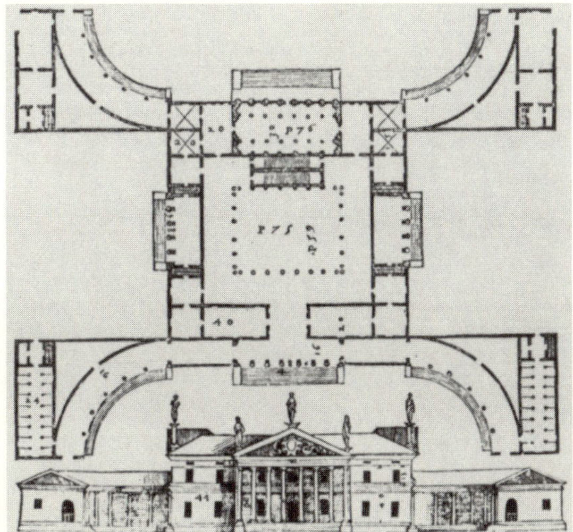

3.5

3.3 A. Palladio, *Casa Private dei Greci* (*The Four Books*)
3.4 A. Palladio, *Piazza dei Greci* (*The Four Books*)
3.5 A. Palladio, Villa Mocenigo sulla Brenta (*The Four Books*)

3.6

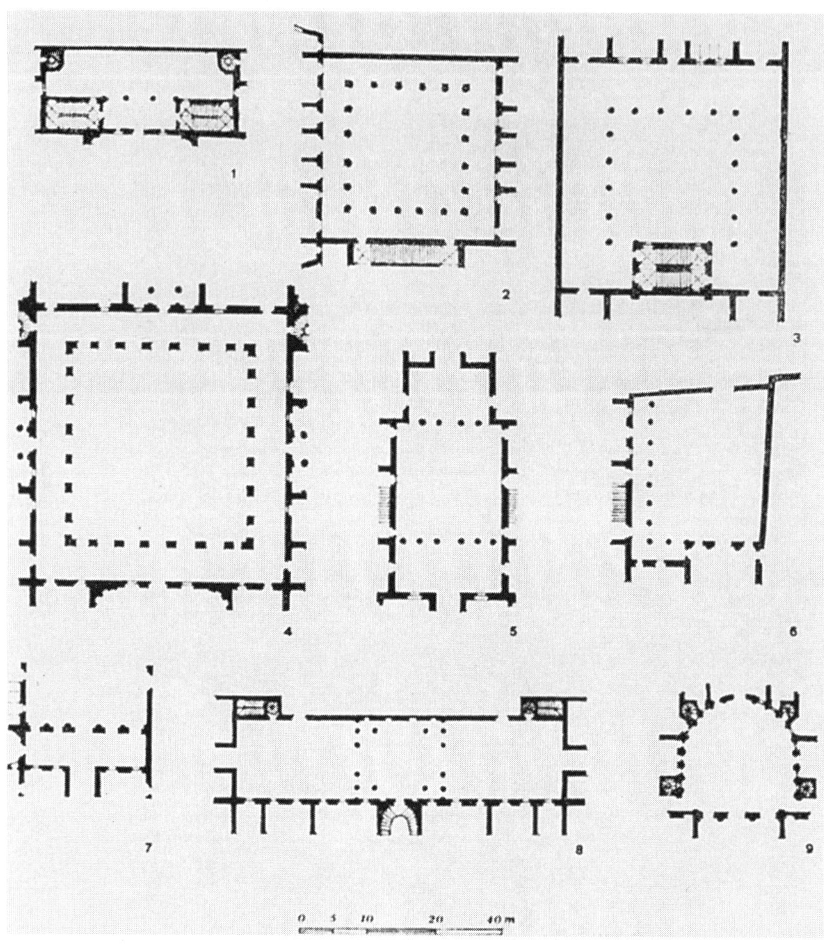

3.6 Courtyards of Palladian palaces: 1.) Palazzo Chiericati; 2.) Palazzo da Porto Festa; 3.) Palazzo Angarano; 4.) Palazzo Thiene; 5.) Palazzo Valmarana; 6.) Palazzo Barbaran da Porto; 7.) Palazzo Capra; 8.) Palazzo Dalla Torre; 9.) Palazzo da Porto Breganze

3.7 A. Palladio, Villa Pisani at Montagnana

3.8 A. Palladio, Palazzo Barbaran da Porto; plan and elevation (*The Four Books*)

3.9 A. Palladio, Palazzo Bonin Longare

3.7

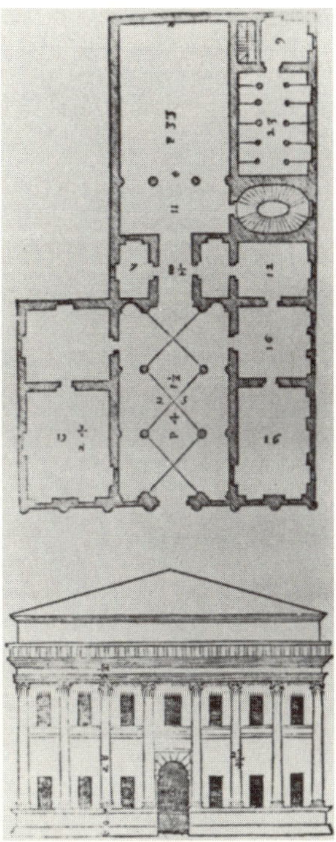

3.8

3.9

3.10

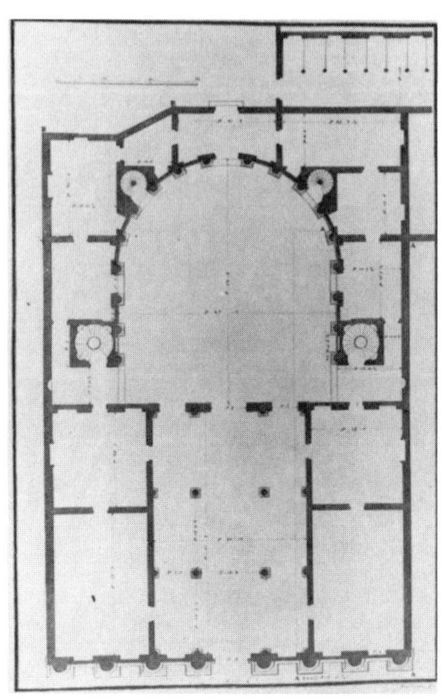
3.11

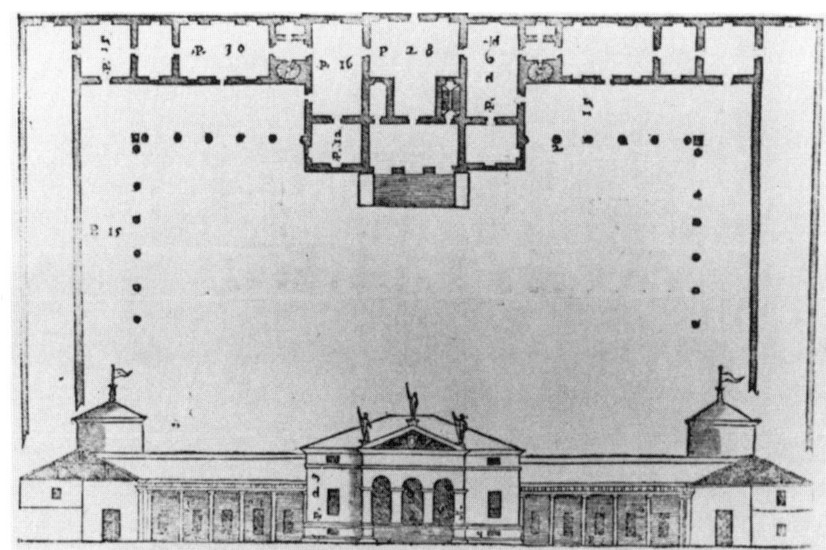
3.12

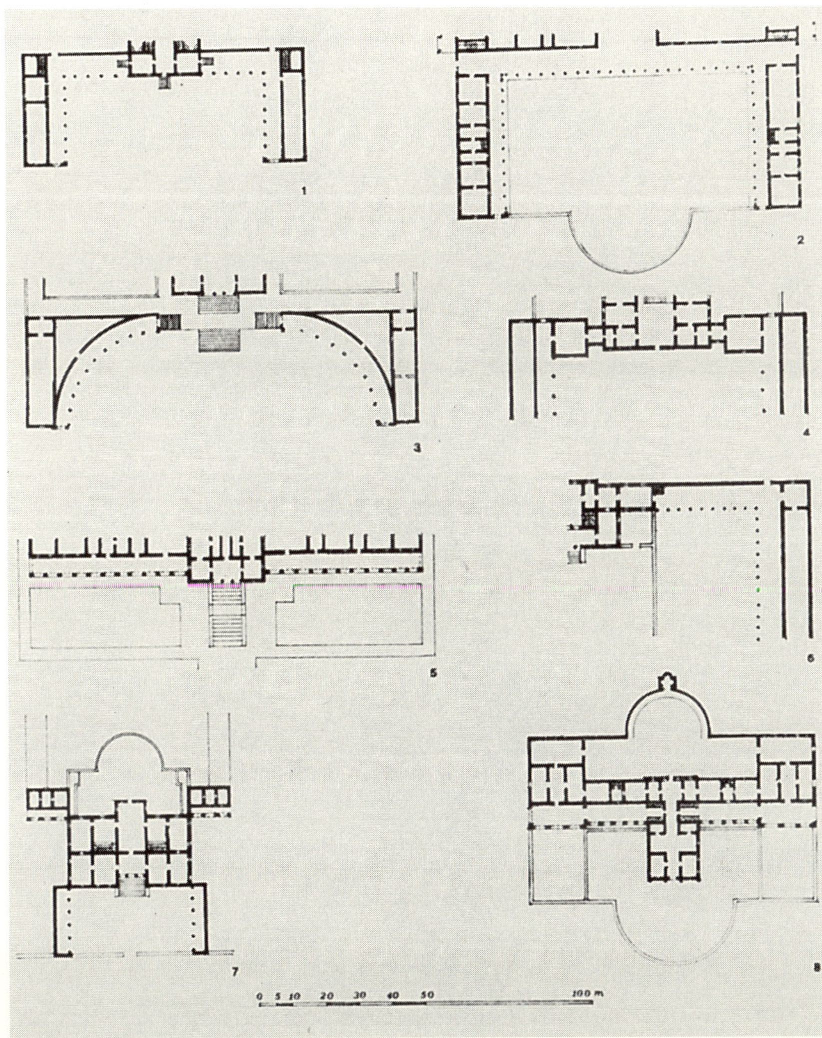

3.13

3.10 A. Palladio, *Piazza dei Greci* (*The Four Books*)

3.11 O. Bertotti Scamozzi, Palazzo Porto Breganze; plan (*Le Fabriche di Palladio*)

3.12 A. Palladio, Villa Saraceno (*The Four Books*)

3.13 Courtyards at Palladian villas: 1.)Villa Zeno; 2.) Villa Repeta; 3.)Villa Badoer; 4.) Villa Mocenigo, Marocco; 5.) Villa Emo; 6.) Villa Pojana; 7.) Villa Godi; 8.) Villa Barbaro

3.14

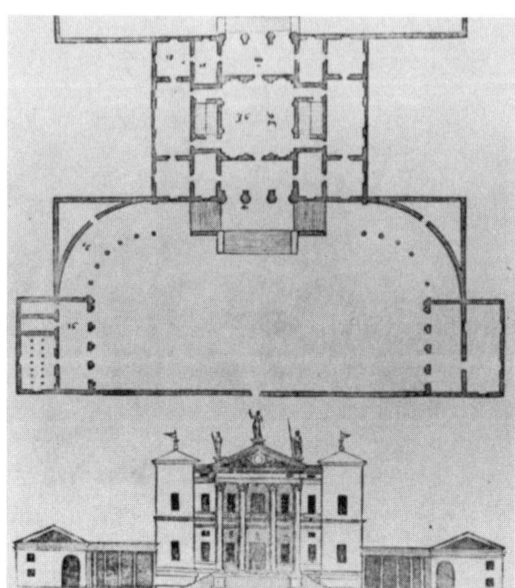

3.15

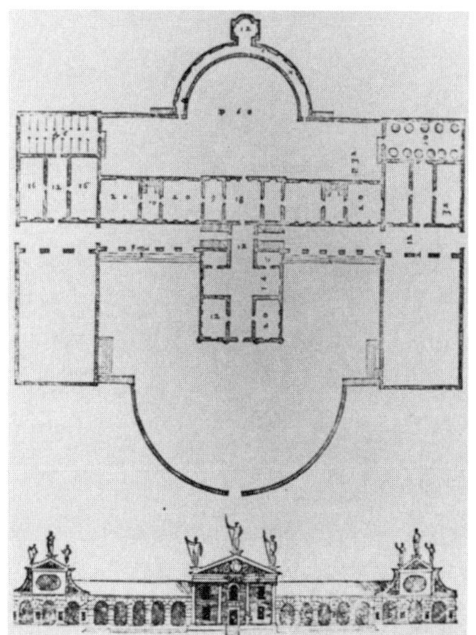

3.14 A. Palladio, Villa Thiene at Cicogna (*The Four Books*)
3.15 A. Palladio, Villa Barbaro (*The Four Books*)

4.1

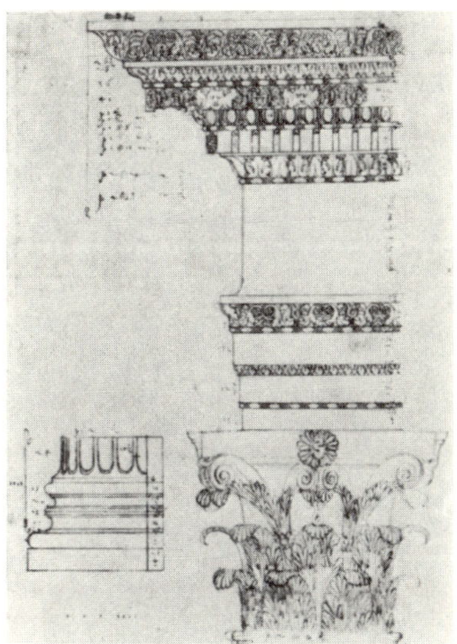

4.3

4.2

4.4

4.1 A. Palladio, Baths of Caracalla; Corinthian capitol and base (*The Four Books*)
4.2 Lord Burlington, Baths of Caracalla; the same Corinthian capitol and base
4.3 A. Palladio, Baths of Caracalla; Corinthian capitol relative trabeation (*The Four Books*)
4.4 Lord Burlington, Baths of Caracalla; the same Corinthian capitol

4.5

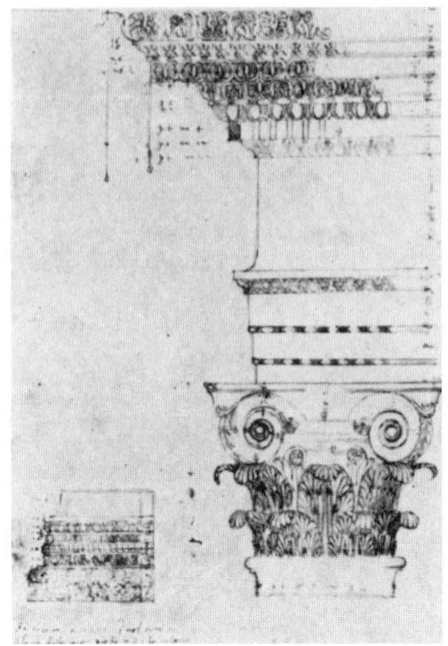

4.7

4.6

4.8

4.5 A. Palladio, Baths of Caracalla; Corinthian capitol with superior trabeation (*The Four Books*)

4.6 Lord Burlington, Baths of Caracalla; the same Corinthian capitol

4.7 A. Palladio, Baths of Caracalla; composite capitol and very decorated column (*The Four Books*)

4.8 Lord Burlington, Baths of Caracalla; the same coposite capitol

4.9

4.11

4.10

4.12

4.9 A. Palladio, Baths of Caracalla; capitol with relative trabeations (*The Four Books*)
4.10 Lord Burlington, Baths of Caracalla; the same capitol
4.11 Lord Burlington, composite capitol
4.12 A. Palladio, Baths of Caracalla (*The Four Books*)

4.13

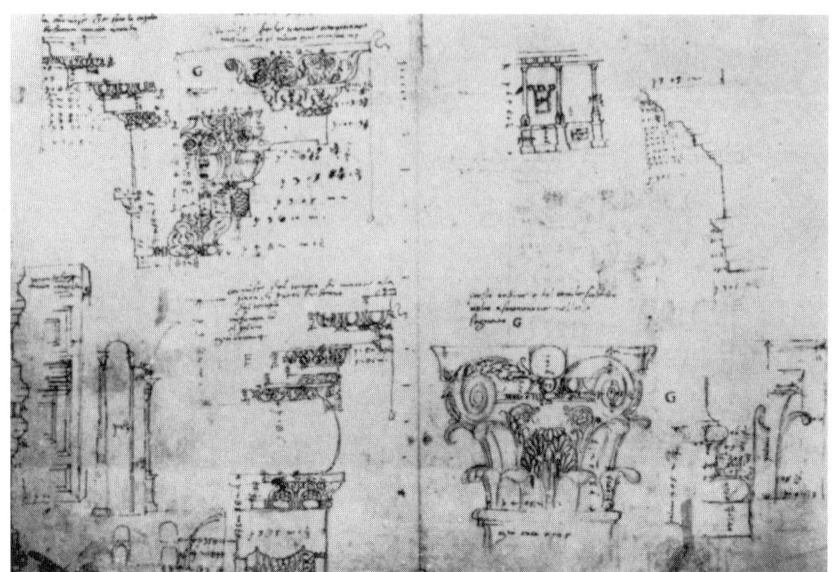

4.14

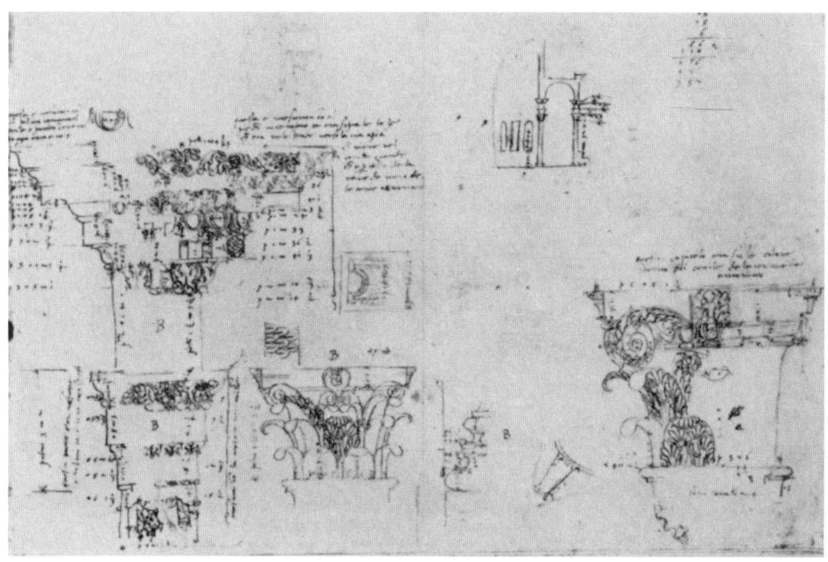

4.13 A. Palladio, Baths of Caracalla; schemes of capitols not reproduced by Lord Burlington

4.14 A. Palladio, Baths of Caracalla; schemes of capitols not reproduced by Lord Burlington

5.1

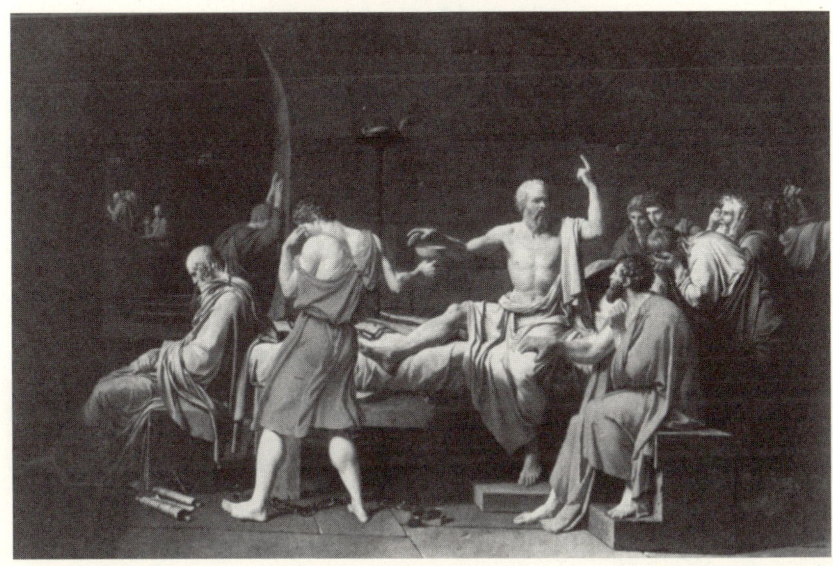

5.2

5.1 A. Canova, "Hercules and Lichas"
5.2 J. L. David, "The Death of Socrates"

6.1

6.2
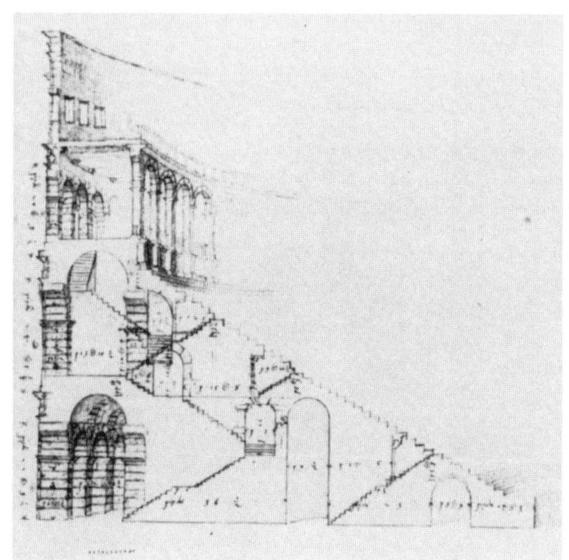

6.1 A. Palladio, Palazzo Civena
6.2 A. Palladio, perspective section of the Roman Theatre, Verona

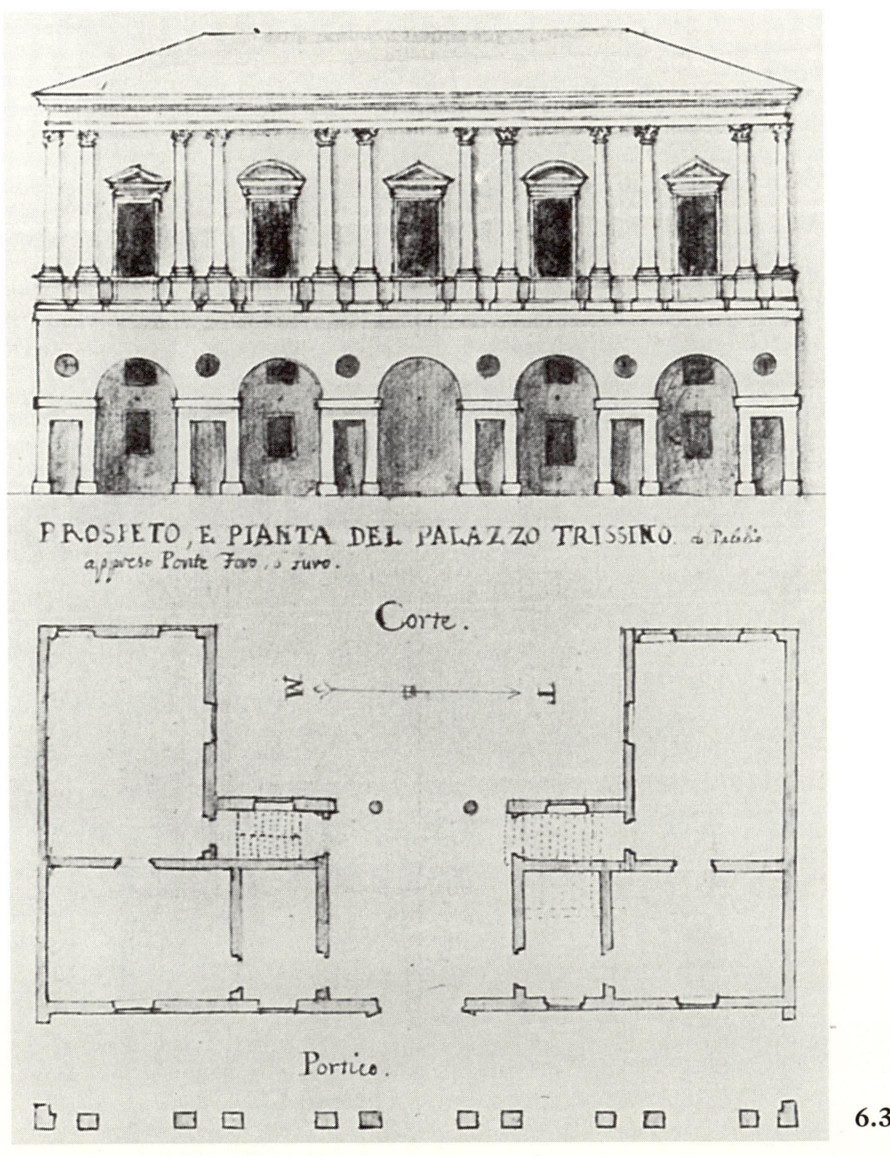

6.3

6.3 A. Palladio, Palazzo Civena; façade and plan (CISA)

6.4 

6.5 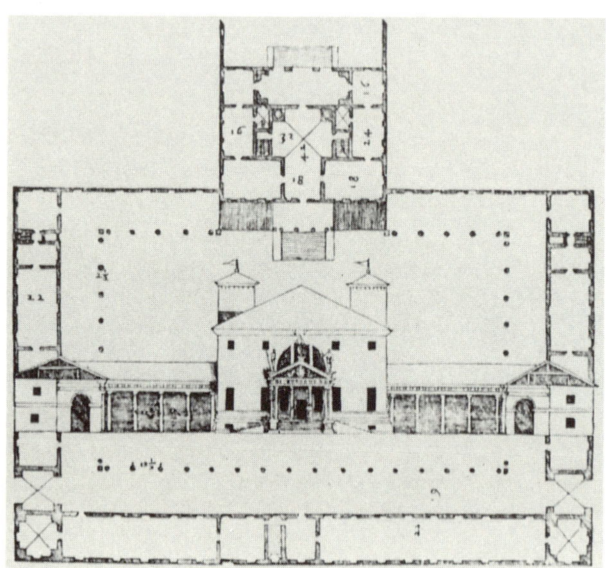

6.4 A. Palladio, Villa Pisani at Bagnolo
6.5 A. Palladio, Villa Pisani at Bagnolo; plan and elevation (*The Four Books*)

6.6

6.7

6.6 A. Palladio, Villa Valmarana at Vigardolo; plan and façade
6.7 A. Palladio, Villa Valmarana at Vigardolo; detail of Serlian entrance

7.1

7.2

7.1 A. Palladio, Church of the Redentore; transverse section by L. Gradis (Correr Museum)

7.2 A. Palladio, Church of the Redentore; aerial

7.3

7.4

7.5

7.3 A. Palladio, Basilica of Vicenza; detail
7.4 A. Palladio, Villa Emo; view from interior to countryside
7.5 A. Palladio, Villa Rotonda; view from interior to countryside

7.6 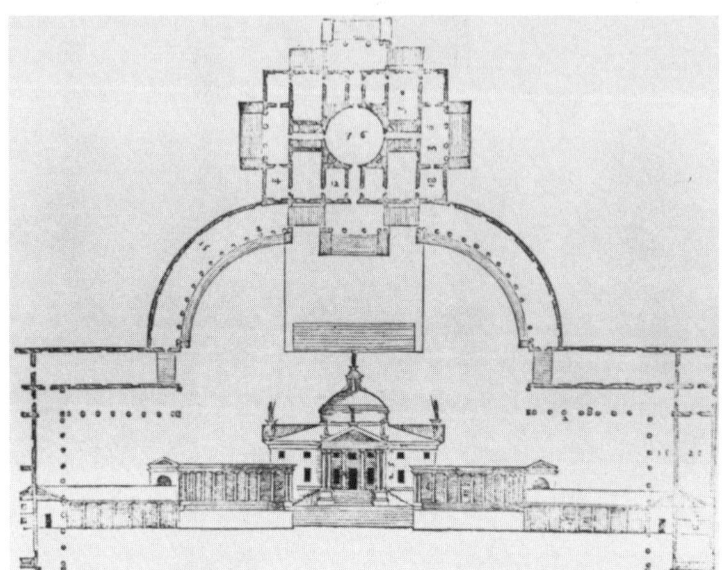

7.7 

7.6 A. Palladio, Villa Trissino at Meledo (*The Four Books*)
7.7 P. Veronese, Villa Barbaro; fresco of Roman ruin

7.8

8.1

7.8 A. Palladio, Villa Rotonda; southwest façade
8.1 A. Palladio, Villa Rotonda; view from the west

8.2

8.3

8.2 A. Palladio, Villa Rotonda; central room
8.3 A. Palladio, Baptistry of Constantine; plan and section

8.4

8.5

8.4 A. Palladio, Basilica of Vicenza; detail
8.5 A. Palladio, Teatro Olimpico; proscenium and auditorium

8.6

8.7

8.6 "Pope's Villa at Twickenham" (Paul Mellon Center for British Arts, Yale University)

8.7 A. Palladio, Palazzo Valmarana (*The Four Books*)

8.8

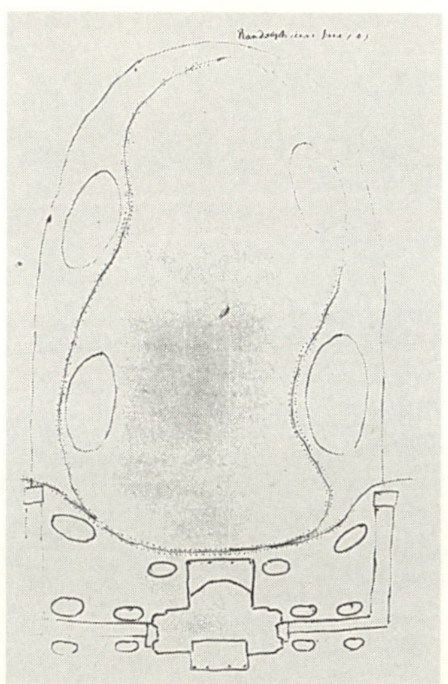

8.9

8.8 T. Jefferson, Monticello; façade of c. 1771 version (Massachusetts Historical Society, Coolidge Collection)

8.9 T. Jefferson, Monticello; sketch of gardens and flower bed of 1807 (Massachusetts Historical Society, Coolidge Collection)

8.10

8.11

8.10 A. Palladio, Villa Barbaro; view with landscape
8.11 G. A. Canal (called Caneletto), "Fantasy of the Ideal Palladian City"